101 Reading Activities™

A Multisensory Approach

Abigail Hanrahan
Catherine McSweeny

Skills:	Phonological Awareness Reading Comprehension
Ages:	6 through 12
Grades:	1 through 7

LinguiSystems, Inc.
3100 4th Avenue
East Moline, IL 61244-9700

1-800-PRO IDEA
1-800-776-4332

FAX: 1-800-577-4555
E-mail: service@linguisystems.com
Web: www.linguisystems.com

TDD: 1-800-933-8331
(for those with hearing impairments)

Printed in the U.S.A.

ISBN 0-7606-0498-3

About the Authors

Abby and Cathy

Abigail Hanrahan, M.A., has been teaching reading at Eagle Hill School, Greenwich, for over 15 years. She lives in Greenwich with her husband, Packy, and their two children, Maddy and Patrick. This is her first publication with LinguiSystems.

Catherine McSweeny, M.A., is teaching at the Lab School of Washington in Washington, D.C. She has taught reading for nine years to students with learning disabilities. She lives in D.C., and this is her first publication with LinguiSystems.

Dedication

To Eagle Hill School,

For inspiring the passion to teach
And the joy of collaboration

To Packy and Paul,

For knowing that we could

Original Illustrations by Margaret Warner

Clip art © 2003 www.arttoday.com

Cover design by Mike Paustian

Table of Contents

Introduction 5

Chapter 1: Phonemic Awareness 9

This chapter will be particularly useful to early elementary teachers or professionals working with children who are not making progress in reading. Many of these activities are foundational activities for acquiring reading skills. The activities in this chapter include rhyme, phoneme counting, segmenting, deleting, and substituting and discriminating sounds. Many of the activities can be modified to address spelling skills.

Chapter 2: Decoding 53

The activities in this section target basic decoding skills as well as strategies to read multisyllabic words. The activities address sound/symbol relationships for single-syllable words as well as syllabication and structural analysis strategies.

Chapter 3: Automaticity and Fluency 88

This chapter emphasizes the importance of developing these skills with the goal of creating fluent readers. Many students who have mastered the decoding process still struggle with these skills. *Automaticity* and *fluency* are defined in the chapter and appropriate activities are detailed.

Chapter 4: Reading Comprehension 120

This chapter is divided into activities for before reading, during reading, and after reading. These activities are applicable to both narrative and expository text. This chapter will be useful for students who are beginning to read for meaning and for those who are fluent readers.

Appendix 176

References 179

Introduction

While current research clearly supports using a multisensory, structured approach to teaching reading, many children who struggle with the decoding process lose interest and motivation in learning to read. Students who have difficulty acquiring decoding skills need multiple experiences and activities in order to develop their skills in the essential areas of phonemic awareness, decoding, automaticity, and fluency. Educators and parents need to offer repeated and various concrete experiences that will allow students to improve their phonemic awareness and develop a foundation for decoding skills.

To maintain students' motivation and interest, educators also need to help students apply these basic skills to uncontrolled "real-life" reading material and literature. However, maintaining students' motivation, especially for older children who struggle with reading, remains a challenge for teachers. Mastering essential skills often requires repeated drill and practice, which can diminish students' interest in learning to read. Providing practice in a variety of multisensory activities will promote their enthusiasm while reinforcing these essential skills.

Words need to be drilled in isolation before they can be incorporated into controlled text. Increased automaticity and reading fluency will come as a result of this continued practice, but this practice does not have to be boring. You need to have flexibility in deciding what methods to utilize to teach specific reading skills and at what rate you will instruct those skills. In addition, you need to incorporate supplementary materials to reinforce basic skills in order to give older readers exposure to more sophisticated reading materials.

Professionals working with students with reading disabilities face an ongoing challenge of keeping their instruction motivating while following a structured, sequential reading program that is necessary for their students' skill development. Learning how to read can be a challenging hurdle for many students. Familiarizing yourself with multisensory techniques and motivating materials will empower you to help your students meet this challenge.

How to Use this Book

This book is designed to cover a variety of reading skills. The activities are appropriate for a wide range of ages; select the age-appropriate activities throughout the book for your students. You can also modify many of the activities to meet the specific needs of your students.

This book is organized with a hierarchy of skills in mind; however, you don't need to complete one section of activities before moving on to the next. For example, you can address automaticity while working on basic decoding skills. Similarly, all readers will benefit from instruction in comprehension skills.

Each chapter begins with a brief overview, followed by activities that target specific areas of reading instruction. Worksheets, word lists, and extension activities reinforce the objectives for specific tasks.

This book is divided into four major sections:

Chapter 1 focuses on phonemic awareness skills. This chapter will be particularly useful to early elementary teachers or professionals working with children who are not making progress in reading. Many of these activities are foundational activities for acquiring reading skills. The activities in this chapter include rhyme, phoneme counting, segmenting, deleting, and substituting and discriminating sounds. Many of the activities can be modified to address spelling skills.

Chapter 2 describes a variety of activities to teach and reinforce decoding skills. The activities in this section target basic decoding skills as well as strategies to read multisyllabic words. The activities address sound/symbol relationships for single-syllable words as well as syllabication and structural analysis strategies.

Chapter 3 is devoted to ideas to improve automaticity and fluency. This chapter emphasizes the importance of developing these skills with the goal of creating fluent readers. Many students who have mastered the decoding process still struggle with these skills. *Automaticity* and *fluency* are defined in the chapter and appropriate activities are detailed.

Chapter 4 focuses on reading comprehension. This chapter is divided into activities for before reading, during reading, and after reading. These activities are applicable to both narrative and expository text. This chapter will be useful for students who are beginning to read for meaning and for those who are fluent readers.

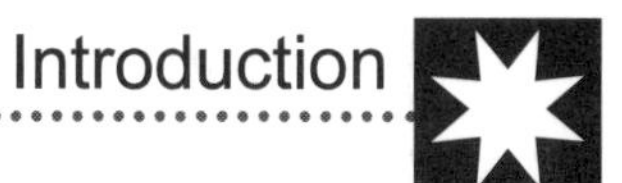

Strategies for Maintaining Motivation

➥ **Personalize the material whenever possible.**

Students respond to their names and personal information. Rewrite stories, worksheets, and practice exercises to include your students' names, addresses, interests, friends, favorite foods, activities, pets, etc. This rewriting will improve students' sight-word vocabulary as well as boost students' enthusiasm about their reading.

Choose materials that are of interest to the students. For example, if you are using a reading program, choose the stories that match your students' interests. This selection process can be a challenge at times. Developing your own library of high-interest stories can be helpful.

➥ **Make the material as sophisticated as possible.**

Supplement and extend stories by using books and resources, including the Internet. For example, if you are reading a story about the sea, require the students to do a mini-report on a marine animal. This strategy is especially important for older readers to help them develop good study skills and to gain valuable background knowledge.

Use "real world" materials, such as newspapers, train schedules, magazines, and menus. Having classroom subscriptions to the local paper as well as age-appropriate magazines and/or comic books will encourage students to apply their skills. In doing so, students learn that reading is not something that just occurs within a classroom; it is a life skill that enables them to gather all sorts of information.

Use materials that may be above students' reading levels to provide visual reinforcement of information. You may need to read such material aloud.

➥ **Encourage independent reading.**

Use the "five-finger rule" to help your students determine if the book is the right level. The students read a page independently. If they come across five difficult words, they should choose an easier book.

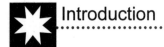

Set challenges and goals. These challenges can be for the whole class or for individuals. Goals can be set for the number of books or the number of pages. The students can also challenge **you**! This challenge is a great way to motivate your students to read over the vacation time. See Appendix A, page 177, and Appendix B, page 178, for examples.

Keep a "Read for 100 Chart" on which students draw a book each time they finish reading one. When the chart is filled with 100 books the students have read, have a book celebration, a "100th Book Party." The students can come to school dressed in their comfiest clothes and hear books read to them, listen to books on tape, and watch videos that are based on books, such as *Charlie and the Chocolate Factory*, *Stone Fox*, and *White Fang*. Involve the students in planning the celebration and invite guest readers, such as the principal, to come and read their favorite books.

Organize "Book Chats" within your class or combine with other classes. Each student has the opportunity to review a book she is currently reading. This is a wonderful way for students to share their enthusiasm for new titles. You can keep an ongoing record of all the books reviewed throughout the year and distribute the list to the students at the end of the year. This list provides a great summer reading guide for the students.

This book is a compilation of all the things we do with students to keep them motivated to read. We hope you find these activities useful when working with your students, but mostly, we hope you have fun and that reading continues to be an enjoyable process for your students.

Abby and Cathy

1 Phonemic Awareness

Research indicates that phonemic awareness is a necessary foundation for acquiring reading skills (Lyon, 1999). Many students who struggle with the reading process lack these basic skills. Using an integrated approach that includes phonics-based activities as well as stories is an effective teaching method. These activities should not be used in isolation. Carefully planned lessons can incorporate phonemic awareness activities to use concurrently with reading instruction.

Phonemic awareness skills should be taught purposefully. Students need to understand how these skills will help their reading. Purposeful activities can act as a springboard to word attack skills and ultimately lead to reading fluency.

Use the activities listed below at the beginning of a reading or spelling lesson. In addition, reinforce these activities wherever and whenever possible.

Many of the following activities include word lists. The words are organized in a hierarchy based on developing decoding skills. The lists include the areas listed below.

- ✓ consonant-vowel-consonant words
- ✓ words that include consonant digraphs and blends
- ✓ silent *e* words
- ✓ words that contain vowel teams and *r*-controlled vowels
- ✓ diphthongs
- ✓ phonetically controlled, multisyllabic words

Magic Box

On the following pages, you will find lots of fun activities to promote reading skills. We recommend assembling a box (a shoe box works well) containing the following items to keep in your classroom. These items will come in handy with many of our activities.

- ✓ Beanbag or Beanie Baby
- ✓ Craft sticks
- ✓ Dice
- ✓ Plastic chips or pennies for phoneme counting and games
- ✓ Game pieces
- ✓ Play-Doh
- ✓ Shaving cream
- ✓ Timer or stopwatch
- ✓ Small cardboard or wooden block to cover or label for question cube activities
- ✓ Spinner
- ✓ Index cards
- ✓ *EZC Reader* by Really Good Stuff (card with a window cutout for tracking purposes)

Rhyme

Many children learn the concept of rhyme at an early age through nursery rhymes, stories, and songs. However, difficulty with rhyming activities is an early indication of potential reading difficulties. Rhyming demonstrates a child's ability to play with language. Students need to understand that many words follow a pattern (e.g., *mop, hop, flop*) so that they can generalize their knowledge base of words. To do this generalizing, though, students need to be able to manipulate sounds; that is why structured phonemic activities that include rhyme are critical. Listed on the following pages are several activities that will help students learn to play with language.

Rhyme Toss

Objective: Students will produce words that rhyme with a given word. For the extension activity, a secondary goal would be having the students remember, retain, and repeat the list of rhyming words as it accumulates.

Materials: Tennis ball, beanbag, or Beanie Baby
Word lists (see pages 12-13)

What to Do: This game starts with all the students standing in a circle. Begin by saying a word, such as *hand*. Then toss a ball to the student on your right. That person adds a rhyming word, such as *sand*. The game continues with each student passing the ball. A player is out if he does not produce a rhyming word in a reasonable amount of time or if he repeats a word that has already been used. When a student is out, he sits. The game ends when all possible rhyming words have been used or when only one person is left standing.

Some students may have a hard time coming up with a rhyming word. It may be helpful to cue them to use the alphabet (posted in your classroom) and to teach them how to change the beginning sound to form a new rhyming word. You can decide whether nonsense words can be used during the game.

Extension Activity

Add a "memory challenge" to the game. Each player repeats the word(s) from the previous student(s), then adds his own word. A player is out when he misses a word.

This is a good activity for students who need to work on improving short-term memory.

Word Lists for Rhyme Games

One-Syllable Words with Short Vowels and Ending Blends/Digraphs

top	fit	rack
cub	send	tan
hip	hot	beg
rug	stamp	gash
lunch	best	milk
lump	long	hunt
shop	wing	ham
witch	batch	sang
link	last	miss
fall	will	list

One-Syllable Words with R-Controlled Vowels

far	card	dart
park	arm	squirm
burn	shirt	fork
cord	short	bird

Long Vowels/Diphthongs

tape	make	name	play
taste	train	pail	trade
light	line	glide	time
pile	fire	life	fly
street	mean	read	beep
fear	leave	grease	me
hope	road	float	broke
coast	dome	groan	bow
use	tube	rude	cute
room	booth	noon	rude
proud	found	shout	hour
howl	toy	broil	town
caught	shower	draw	fowl

Two-Syllable Words

handy	jolly	chilly
hairy	funny	floppy
flurry	madly	sitting
leaking	weeping	trying
trouble	dimmer	nation
flower	wiper	jacket
later	letter	shiny
eating	able	giggle
marry	bacon	floating
mumble	pinches	selling
butter	tougher	shaker
middle	wonder	lovely

Thumbs

Objective: Students will determine whether pairs of words rhyme or not.

Materials: Desks or tables
Word list (see below and page 15)

What to Do: Have all the students put their heads on their desks, covering their eyes. Each student keeps one hand out on the desk. Say a pair of words, such as *slip, trip.* Each student holds a thumb "up" if the words rhyme or a thumb "down" if the words do not rhyme, such as *flip, trap.*

Word Pairs

sip, trip *yes*

fit, rat *no*

win, spin *yes*

long, wrong *yes*

hand, bend *no*

milk, silk *yes*

hunt, tint *no*

think, thing *no*

most, boast *yes*

cool, food *no*

weep, sheet *no*

winner, spinner *yes*

hitting, winning *no*

letter, litter *no*

sing, fling *yes*

sick, peck *no*

rest, test *yes*

lock, tuck *no*

hang, sprang *yes*

tusk, must *no*

sent, wink *no*

float, spoke *no*

spool, fool *yes*

dream, speed *no*

grow, snow *yes*

flower, tower *yes*

loud, shout *no*

store, more *yes*

Extension Activity

Say three words, two of which rhyme, such as *flip, trip, flap*. Then repeat the three words and have the students put their thumbs down when they hear the non-rhyming word. You can then ask a student to explain why the word doesn't rhyme, such as "*Flap* doesn't rhyme because the vowel sound is different."

Words for Extension Activity

read, feed, **queen**

please, **heave**, tease

beam, **lean**, steam

pear, bear, **door**

age, strange, change

last, paste, taste

wink, **thing**, pink

taken, bacon, **shaker**

winning, spinning, **fitting**

letter, suffer, rougher

annoy, destroy, **avoid**

bumper, **hunger**, thumper

out, pout, **moat**

riddle, **ripple**, middle

shiny, tiny, **tidy**

wiggle, giggle, **little**

butter, **wetter**, flutter

scribble, able, stable

eating, **speaking**, seating

bundle, grumble, mumble

selling, smelling, **filling**

flinches, pinches, **lunches**

Who's Got the Rhyme?

Objective: Students identify rhyming words

Materials: Picture cards (see pages 18-21)

Magazine clippings

Common objects such as those below to present in groups of up to six at a time:

candle	pen	card
dice	toy car	rubber band
tape	scissors	shell
can	thumbtack	flower
coin	paper clip	clock

What to Do: The activity begins with an assortment of picture cards (copy and cut apart the pictures from pages 18-21) or common objects spread out on a table or on the floor. The students sit in a circle around the objects. Each student takes an even number of pictures or objects and sets them in front of him.

Call out a word, such as *handle*. The student who has the rhyming object or picture holds it up in the air, calling out the rhyming words ("I have a candle. That rhymes with *handle*.") The activity continues until you have used all of the pictures or objects.

Use these words with the pictures on page 18.

key (bee)	berries (cherries)	word (bird)
fuss (bus)	hike (bike)	trees (cheese)
train (plane)	ice (dice)	hat (cat)
proud (cloud)	car (star)	paddle (saddle)

Use these words with the pictures on page 19.

fun (sun)	slight (kite)	course (horse)
smuggle (juggle)	fellow (yellow)	tickle (nickel)
pair (chair)	time (dime)	long (strong)
thank (tank)	think (sink)	smart (dart)

Use these words with the pictures on page 20.

hard (card)	tire (fire)	pile (smile)
handy (candy)	shade (braid)	dunk (trunk)
wiggle (giggle)	sweet (feet)	ground (pound)
fail (tail)	charm (farm)	dirt (shirt)

Use these words with the pictures on page 21.

mouse (house)	coast (toast)	toad (road)
feel (wheel)	pain (rain)	sharp (harp)
wait (bait)	root (boot)	join (coin)
proud (loud)	twist (fist)	swing (ring)

Extension Activity

Once the students have become more proficient with the rhyming task, have the students take turns calling out a stimulus word, or have the students write the rhyming words on a piece of paper and see how many more rhyming words they can come up with.

Copy these pictures. Cut them apart to use with *Who's Got the Rhyme?*, pages 16-17.

bee	 cherries	 bird
bus	 bike	 cheese
 plane	 dice	 cat
 cloud	 star	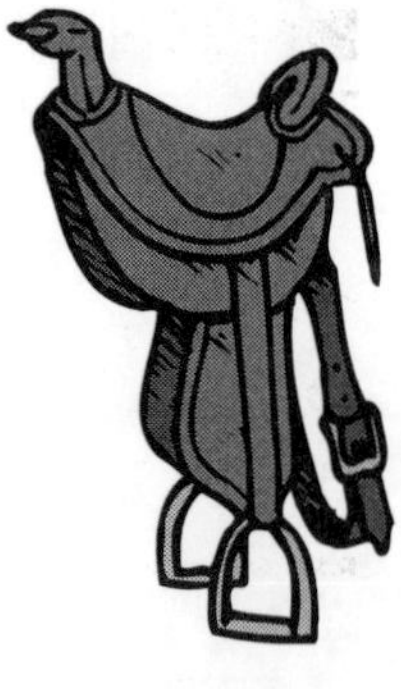 saddle

Copy these pictures. Cut them apart to use with *Who's Got the Rhyme?*, pages 16-17.

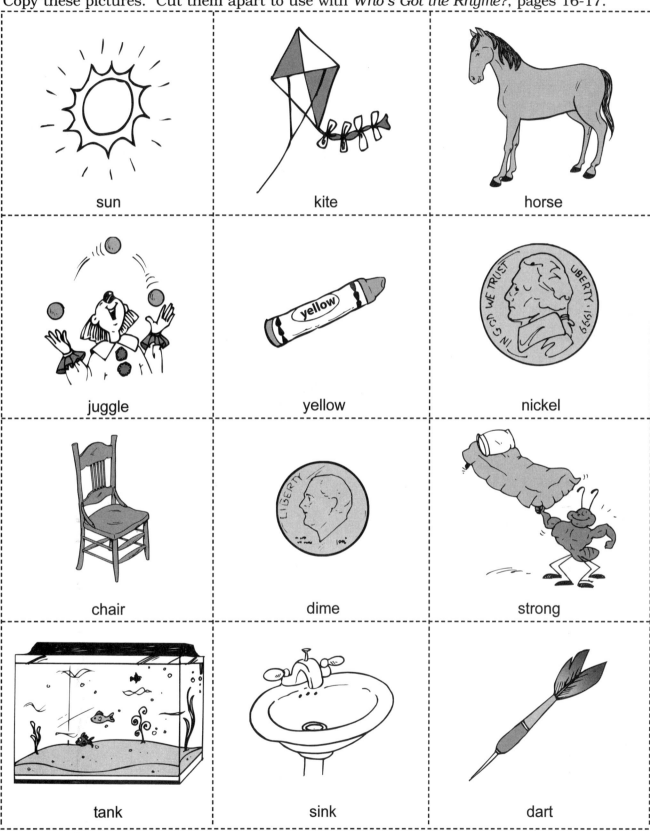

sun	 kite	 horse
 juggle	 yellow	nickel
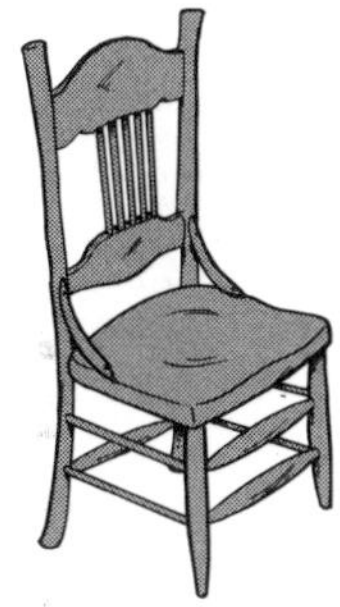 chair	dime	 strong
 tank	 sink	 dart

Chapter 1: Phonemic Awareness

Copy these pictures. Cut them apart to use with *Who's Got the Rhyme?*, pages 16-17.

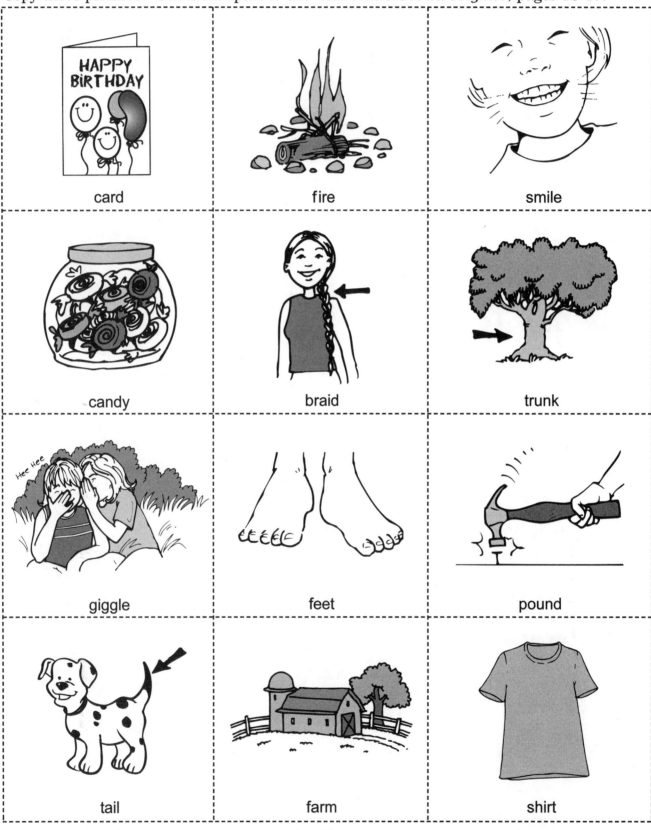

card	fire	smile
candy	braid	trunk
giggle	feet	pound
tail	farm	shirt

Copy these pictures. Cut them apart to use with *Who's Got the Rhyme?*, pages 16-17.

house	 toast	 road
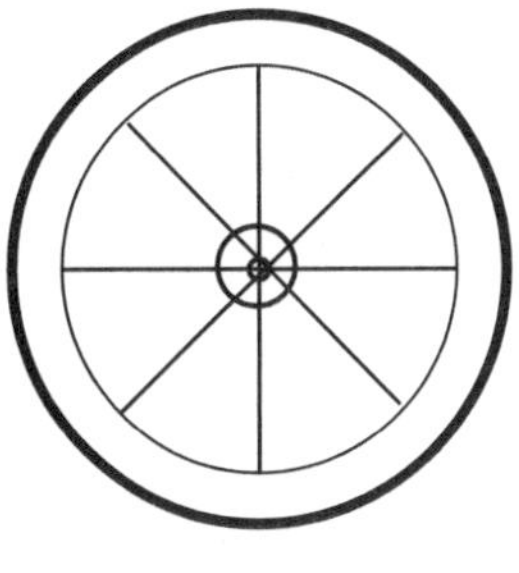 wheel	 rain	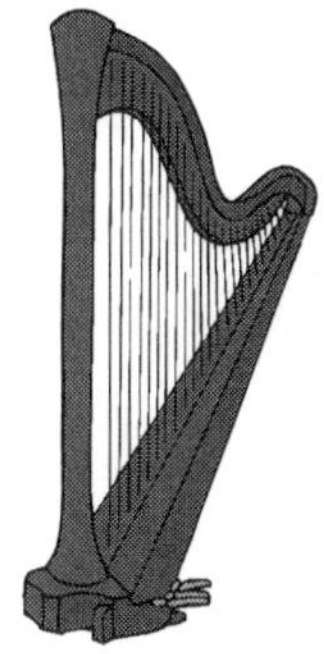 harp
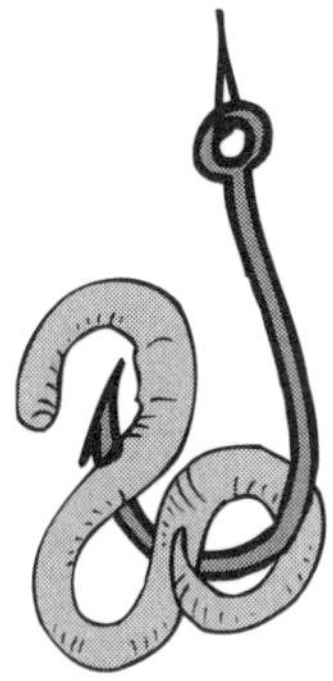 bait	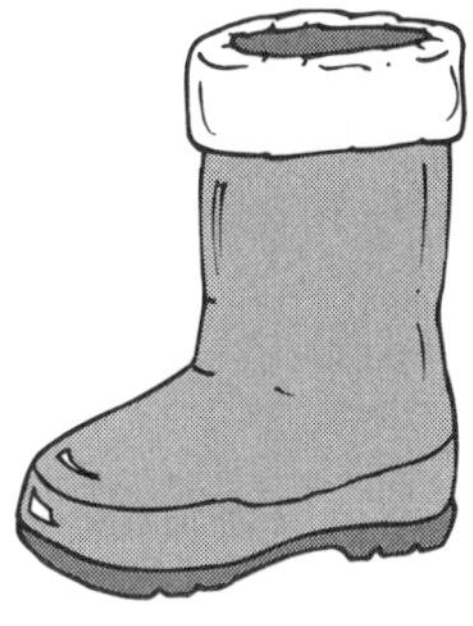 boot	 coin
 loud	 fist	 ring

Rhyming "I Spy"

Objective: When given a stimulus word, the students will produce a rhyming word from their environment or from a picture.

Materials: None (or picture scenes)

What to Do: This is a rhyming version of the old favorite "I Spy." The game is played using the classroom environment, a picture from a magazine, or a poster of a scene.

Begin by saying, "I spy something that rhymes with *dock.*" A student answers, "Clock!"

If a student is having great difficulty with rhyming, you can cue her by saying, "I'm looking for something on the floor that rhymes with ____." Alternatively, you can simply use more obvious things from the room or the picture. Naming the target items in the room or the picture before beginning the game may also help the student be more successful in detecting rhyming words.

You can give the more challenging examples (two-syllable words) to the students who are more proficient in rhyming.

Extension Activity

To provide a greater challenge, have your students take turns being the teacher and calling out the stimulus words.

Ring Around the Rhyme

Objective: Students will generate a list of rhyming words.

Materials: Table or desks, arranged in a circle
Tape player with music
Paper for writing word lists (at lease one sheet per student)
Markers or pens with different ink colors (one per student)

What to Do: This activity is a new twist on "Musical Chairs." Give each student a different color marker or pen to write with. Around a table (or on desks arranged in a circle), put papers with a single word at the top of each one. Some example words are listed below.

Short-Vowel Words	*Long-Vowel Words*	*Diphthong Words*
pick	street	oil
bed	take	coin
stack	pile	sound
sock	rain	loud
hug	coast	now
hang	name	toy
then	fuse	town
kiss	time	shout
thing	road	noise
pitch	case	law
match	nice	bought
lunch	page	hour
cash	hide	owl
wish	light	house

Two-Syllable Words

letter	silly	funny
sweeter	trying	trouble
dimmer	nation	flower
wiper	jacket	later

When the music starts, the students move around the circle. When the music stops, the students sit down in front of a paper. The students quickly write a word that rhymes with the word at the top of the paper at their spots.

At the end of several rounds, post the word lists on the wall or chalkboard. Have your students help identify which words to eliminate: words that do not rhyme, words that have been repeated, nonsense words, names, etc. Typically, each student earns credit for words that rhyme even if the words are not spelled correctly because the emphasis for this activity is on rhyming, not spelling.

If all the students use a different color marker during this activity, it will be easy to count up each student's total number of acceptable words at the end of the game. The student with the most credited words wins.

Extension Activity

This activity provides a wonderful opportunity to discuss the spelling options for certain words. For example, if a student writes the word *bate* (*bait*) under the list for words that rhyme with *late*, you can discuss the different spelling for the "*ate*" sound and start a classroom list for future reference.

Word Pattern Categories

Objective: Students will improve their understanding of word patterns.

Materials: One copy of Word Patterns, page 26, per student

What to Do: This activity is simple to set up and easy to modify to suit students' individual needs.

Copy the grid on page 26. At the top of the grid, write three rimes (see the example below). Then copy this grid for each student. (Do this activity on an overhead or as a group the first time to demonstrate.)

Give each student a copy of the grid. Announce a time limit, such as five minutes. Within the time limit, each student completes as much of the grid as she can, filling in only real words. When the time is up, give the students credit (or points) for every spot in the grid completed accurately.

Word Patterns

First Sounds	-og	-ash	-unk
d	dog	dash	dunk
cl	clog	clash	clunk
2-3 syllables	warthog	succotash	preshrunk

Extension Activity

If all the students are using the same grid, each student can take a turn sharing her answers out loud. If any students have the same response, both students must cross out that response. Give credit only for unique responses, thus providing a greater challenge for students to think of uncommon words, such as *succotash*.

Read each word pattern at the top of this grid. Think of words that end with each pattern. Write the beginning sound of each word in the column on the left. Then fill in the grid.

Word Patterns

First Sounds			
2-3 Syllables			
2-3 Syllables			
2-3 Syllables			

Poetry Completion

Objective: Students will improve their understanding of rhyme in the context of poetry. This activity also provides the opportunity to work on developing reading fluency and intonation.

Materials: Poetry books such as those by Shel Silverstein, Jack Prelutsky, and Jane Yolen

For the extension activity (see page 28), you will need large sheets of chart paper or butcher block paper.

What to Do: Reading poetry to kids is a great way of developing their understanding of rhyme as well as intonation and fluency. For this activity, choose a poem and read it, leaving out the rhyming word(s). Have your students complete the lines. Here is an example poem.

The Big Game

The team was in a huddle,
Their feet soaking in a ____. *puddle*

The fans began to grumble
When the player made a ____. *fumble*

There was a mighty scramble,
Since the quarterback took a ____. *gamble*

The ball was thrown at an angle,
And the team landed in a ____. *tangle*

The visitors began to giggle
When their quarterback touched down with a ____. *wiggle*

Extension Activity

Have the students write their own poetry using a list of words from spelling lessons or other areas of the curriculum. For example, the following poem can be used to reinforce *ai*, *a* + silent *e*, and homonyms.

The Three Sailors

There were three sailors who went to **Spain**.
They got out of their ship and took a ____. *train*
In the town there was a **fair**.
They all went to cut their ____. *hair*
At the fair there was a **sale**.
One sailor wanted to read a ____. *tale*
Another sailor could not **wait**
To find a dock and fish with ____. *bait*
Sailor number three had some **mail**
To send to his sister named ____. *Gail*
They had fun at the fair in **Spain**.
It was too bad it had to ____. *rain*

Phoneme Segmenting/Counting

Another essential component to increasing phonemic awareness is the ability to break words into their individual sounds and parts. This is a difficult task for many students and needs to be taught explicitly. Many students simply cannot hear the individual sounds that make up the beginning, middle, and end of words. The activities on the following pages will increase students' awareness of individual sounds within a word. In addition, students who are able to identify individual sounds within a word are better able to spell phonetically controlled words, such as *smash*, *stuck*, *student*, and *rodeo*.

These activities will also provide informal diagnostic information for you as a teacher. For example, a student may struggle with differentiating medial short vowels or may consistently drop the ending sounds of words. These activities will help you pinpoint specific areas that need direct instruction or review.

Sound Tapping

Objective: Students will hear and tap for individual phonemes, thus improving their ability to decode phonetically controlled words.

Materials:
Small pieces of Velcro
Felt squares
Sandpaper
Xylophone or drum
List of nonsense words (see pages 35-37)

What to Do: Provide students with small pieces of Velcro, felt, or sandpaper. Starting with small words (three phonemes), say a word slowly, modeling for the student how to tap out each sound on a separate piece of Velcro. For example, for the word *pet*, the student touches a piece of Velcro for each of the sounds—"*p*," "*e*," "*t*," three sounds. The activity continues building up to longer words with more phonemes.

Having students tap out the sounds of words reinforces phonemic awareness through their senses. Depending on students' interests and needs, have the students use a xylophone or drum to tap out each sound.

Note that attaching Velcro squares or sandpaper circles to your students' desks also works well and is more accessible to students who need this strategy to help them read or spell.

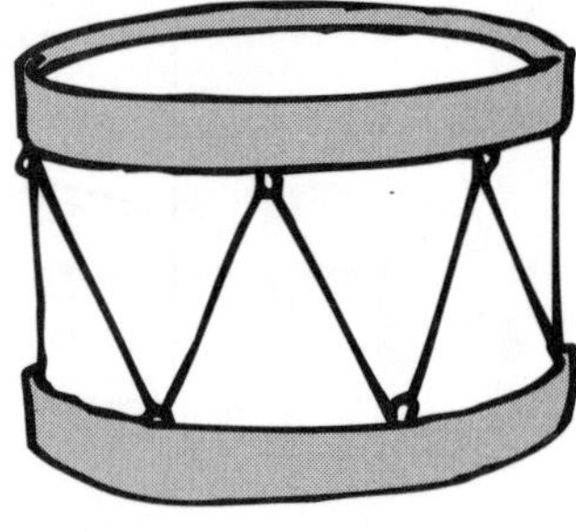

Muffin Tin

Objective: Students will identify the number of individual phonemes within a word.

Materials: Muffin tin
Pennies or chips
List of nonsense words (see pages 35-37)

What to Do: Give the students a muffin tin and several pennies. Starting with small words (three phonemes), demonstrate how to say the word slowly, accentuating each phoneme while dropping a coin into each cup of the tin as you say a phoneme. The students can identify the number of sounds by counting how many cups have been filled with pennies.

Rip Strip

Objective: Students will identify the phonemes in a given word and then blend the phonemes together to reform the word.

Materials: Velcro Rip Strip (see directions and illustrations below)
Strips of fabric 1" x 4" (faux fur works well)
List of nonsense words (see pages 35-37)

What to Do: A Rip Strip is a simple tool to help your students really "hear" the sounds being separated in a word. First put one fabric square on a Rip Strip square for each sound in a word. Say the word. Have a student pull a fabric strip off the Rip Strip as she says each sound in the word. After she has said each phoneme, she should blend the sounds together to say the whole word.

To create a Rip Strip, glue six small squares of Velcro onto a ruler. The fabric strips will stick to the Velcro squares and should be able to be pulled off fairly easily.

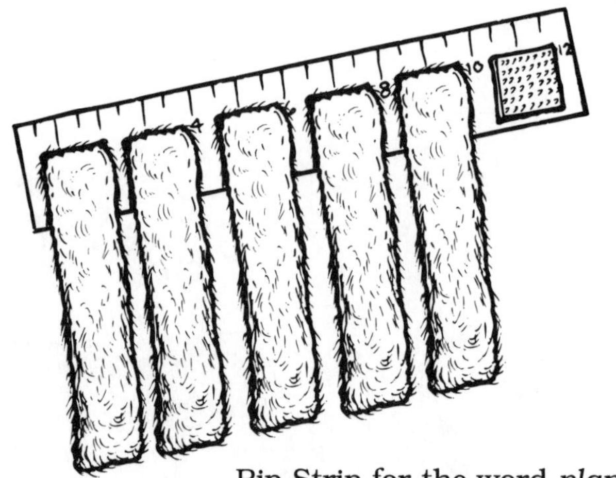

Rip Strip for the word *plant*

Sound Colors

Objective: Students will identify the phonemes in words by writing each sound in a different color.

Materials: Markers, crayons, paints, colored pencils, or colored chalk
Word list

What to Do: Have each student select three different colors; one for the beginning, middle, and ending sounds of words. Give each student a list of words he is learning and have him trace over or rewrite the words, using a color to represent the beginning, middle, and ending sounds of each word. The list below shows words in different shades as examples for this activity.

dash	this	lock
shack	chip	shop
path	chin	fog
cab	rib	knob
lash	ship	knot

Sound Count

Objective: Students will identify the number of phonemes in a word.

Materials: Manipulatives to count word sounds (Velcro strips, chips, etc.)
Markers (different color for each student)
Blank slips of paper
Bowl or bag
List of nonsense words (see pages 35-37)

What to Do: Give your students a word. Have the students use Velcro strips, plastic chips, or whatever manipulative they need to count out the sounds. Each student writes the number of sounds on the slip of paper and puts the paper into a bowl in the center of the table. When everyone has finished, check the slips. Each correct response earns one point. You will know which response belongs to which student by the color of the ink.

In this activity, as with other phoneme counting activities, it may be beneficial to use nonsense words/syllables. Often students have memorized the spelling of many words, and this can confuse students when they try to determine the number of phonemes in a word vs. the number of letters (e.g., *block* has four phonemes but five letters). Refer to the Nonsense Words List and the word cards on pages 35-37 for stimulus words.

Nonsense Words List

Words	Number of Phonemes
Single-syllable	
fim	3
pav	3
lub	3
bef	3
shog	3
meech	3
thit	3
shaid	3
stee	3
toam	3
fost	4
swid	4
shaimp	4
shreb	4
proad	4
fleesh	4
chims	4
plaik	4
sload	4
droob	4
bolp	4
yilk	4
spilm	5
greesk	5
frelp	5
twaist	5
stilk	5
prump	5
groft	5
clend	5

Words	Number of Phonemes
Two-syllable	
vitmus	6
tibbit	5
boskin	6
piplump	7
bancham	6
papline	6
simplam	7
shamka	5
daispin	6
tenblame	7
praiston	7
sindroop	7
tontle	5
hispy	5

The words in this list are printed in boxes on the next two pages. Copy these pages and cut the words apart to use in student activities.

Copy these words. Cut them apart to use for nonsense word activities.

fim	swid
pav	shaimp
lub	shreb
bef	proad
shog	fleesh
meech	chims
thit	plaik
shaid	sload
stee	droob
toam	bolp
fost	yilk

Copy these words. Cut them apart to use for nonsense word activities.

spilm	piplump
greesk	bancham
frelp	papline
twaist	simplam
stilk	shamka
prump	daispin
groft	tenblame
clend	praiston
vitmus	sindroop
tibbit	tontle
boskin	hispy

Phoneme Jump

Objective: Students will separate sounds within a word and count the number of phonemes in a word.

Materials: Masking tape

What to Do: This activity gets students really moving as they "jump out" the sounds in words. Using masking tape, make square boxes on the floor. You can make the same number of square boxes as you have phonemes in a word, or you can make as many square boxes as you want and just have your students do a continual jump around the room.

Either way, once you have set up the masking tape boxes, provide a student with a word and have him "jump out" the sounds while moving from square to square. On the last box, the student should tell you how many sounds are in the word by counting the number of squares he has jumped. For example, in the word *flat*, the student jumps on four boxes, indicating there are four phonemes in the word.

Extension Activity

This activity can often spark an important conversation about words, such as "The word *splash* has six letters, but only five sounds. Why?" It is important for students to recognize that the two letters *sh* make just one sound, as do other letter combinations (digraphs), such as *th*, *ch*, and *ph*.

Karate Kids

Objective: Students will segment all the phonemes or syllables within individual words.

Materials: None

What to Do: Each student stands with her fists out in front of her. Each student is then given a word to "karate chop." The students make one karate chop for each sound in their given word, one "chop" at a time. Below is an example of the "chops" for the word *clap*.

"c"	"l"	"a"	"p"
chop	chop	chop	chop

Extension Activity

You can modify this activity to target specific sounds or the placement of sounds in words. Have your students do small "chops" and then a big "karate chop" when they hit the target sound. For example, if you wanted your student to focus on the ending sounds of words, she could say "*c* - *l* - *a*" and "karate chop" the last sound, "*p*."

Stretch It Out

Objective: Students will identify the number of sounds or syllables in a given word.

Materials: Beanbag, small ball, or Beanie Baby
List of nonsense words (see pages 35-37)

What to Do: Have your students stand and form a circle. Give a stimulus word and pass a beanbag to the first student in the circle. Nonsense words are best because they are harder to visualize, thus the students haven't memorized the number of sounds, or won't confuse the number of letters with number of sounds. The first student in the circle says the word again, emphasizing each phoneme by stretching the word out. He passes a beanbag to the next student, who repeats the word, again stretching it out. This warmup ensures that all students hear each of the sounds or syllables in the word accurately.

Each student takes a turn until the beanbag ends up at the beginning of the circle. Then the first student says only the first sound or syllable of the word, passing the beanbag to the next student. The second student says the second sound or syllable and passes the beanbag to the next student in the circle, and so on. The round ends when all the phonemes or syllables in the word have been accounted for.

B. M. E. (Beginning, Middle, End)

Objective: Students will discriminate where a given sound is located in a word. Students will also compare sounds in words.

Materials: Three cups or small buckets labeled *B*, *M*, and *E*
Small counters (plastic discs, plastic poker chips, or pennies)

What to Do: This activity is designed to help the students identify where the sound is in a given word. Set the three labeled cups or small buckets at the end of a long table or on a student's desk. Give each student a number of small counters.

Say a word, such as *chip*, and ask, "Where do you hear '*ch*' in the word *chip*?" The student tosses a counter into the *B* cup to indicate that the "*ch*" sound is at the beginning of the word *chip*. The game ends when the students have used all of their counters. Below are some example words for this activity.

Where do you hear "*k*" in *track*? *E*
Where do you hear "*t*" in *taken*? *B*
Where do you hear "*d*" in *ladder*? *M*
Where do you hear "*ch*" in *chin*? *B*
Where do you hear "*ch*" in *much*? *E*
Where do you hear "*sh*" in *push*? *E*
Where do you hear "*sh*" in *share*? *B*
Where do you hear "*sh*" in washer? *M*
Where do you hear "*th*" in *this*? *B*
Where do you hear "*th*" in *brother*? *M*
Where do you hear the short "*i*" in *sling*? *M*
Where do you hear the short "*e*" in *ending*? *B*
Where do you hear the long "*e*" in *sleep*? *M*
Where do you hear the long "*a*" in *acorn*? *B*
Where do you hear the long "*o*" in *halo*? *E*

Extension Activity

To modify this activity for phoneme discrimination, ask your students to identify how two words are the same or different, such as, "How are these words the same? *bleach, speak*"

Phoneme Discrimination, Substitution, and Deletion

The ability to discriminate, substitute, and delete sounds is another precursor to acquiring solid reading skills.

Phoneme discrimination is the ability to identify and compare individual sounds in a word or words. Activities for this skill essentially ask students to discern how two words are similar and/or different, such as "How are *chop* and *chip* different/the same?"

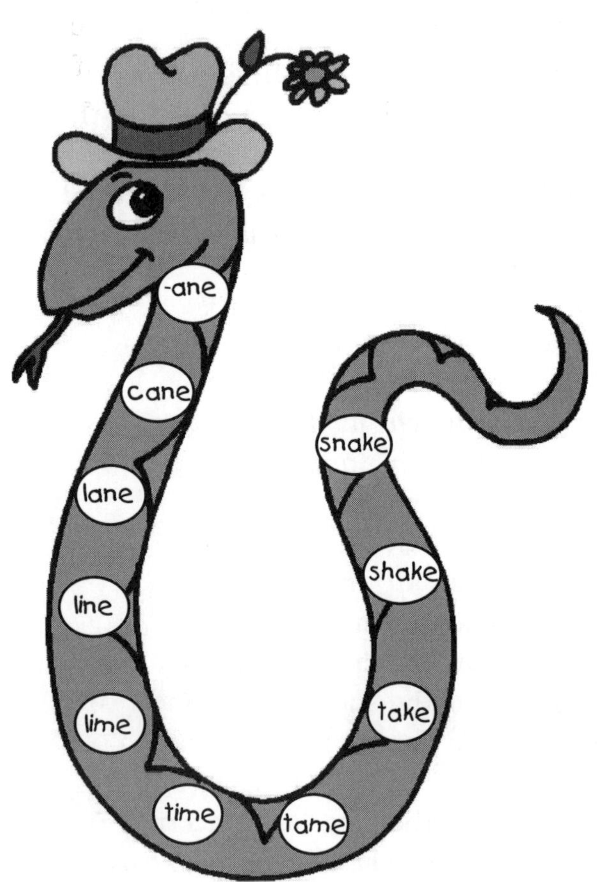

Phoneme substitution is the ability to manipulate sounds within words to form new words. A typical task in this skill area is "Change the '*a*' sound in *stack* to the '*u*' sound. What is the new word?"

Phoneme deletion activities ask the student to omit sounds to make a new word. For example, "Drop the '*s*' sound from *spill*. What is the new word?"

The activities on the following pages engage students in developing these three specific skills.

Stand Up, Sit Down

Objective: Students will identify vowel sounds and discriminate between long and short vowels.

Materials: Five index cards per student, each marked with a vowel
Word list (see below)

What to Do: This activity reinforces vowel identification, and it is also a great activity for students who need to move during a lesson. Give each student five vowel cards. When you call out a word, the students pick up the vowel they hear and stand up if the vowel is long (making their bodies long) or sit down if the vowel is short (making their bodies short). Below are some example words to try.

Short-Vowel Words

back	stock	flat
chop	log	will
blend	hunt	stand
stem	cut	fund
still	milk	drop
spent	spread	tint
clock	fist	last
miss	hush	wet
film	squish	chin
them	help	spread
spot	pest	golf

Long-Vowel Words

slate	steam	speed
nice	race	rope
file	change	sweet
waste	use	spoke
chain	tire	while
greed	quite	stove
mule	name	use
feed	dose	kite
coat	toast	sprite
hope	trade	cute

Tangle

Objective: Students will discriminate vowel sounds or spellings.

Materials: Twister plastic mat or a tablecloth with circles drawn on it

List of words (see page 23) or nonsense words (see pages 35-37)

What to Do: This game is played just like Twister. It is suitable for up to four players. First choose four vowel sounds to feature. Write them in the circles on the mat or tablecloth.

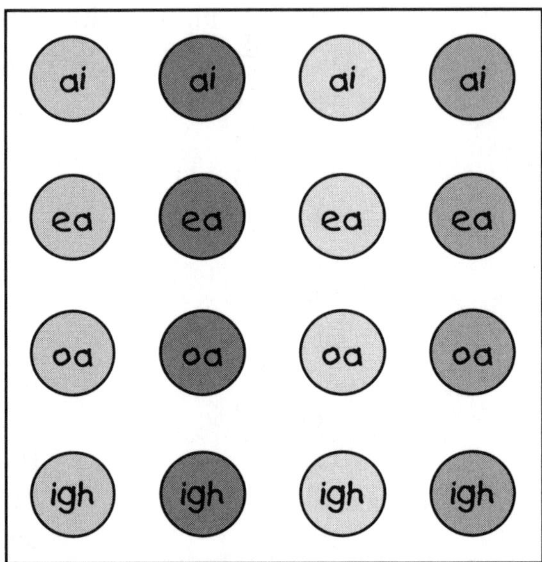

For each turn, call out a word and *left* or *right* and *hand* or *foot (e.g., "Sigh, right, foot."* Each student will place the appropriate foot (or hand) on the circle with the vowel sound in the target word. Students are out when they fall or land on the wrong vowel. The last remaining student wins the game.

Extension Activity

Label the circles with different spellings of the same sound, such as *ay*, *a-e*, *ai*, and *eigh*. The students then have to visualize the word in order to put their feet or hands on the right spot.

Toss a Vowel

Objective: Students will discriminate vowel sounds.

Materials: Five paper cups or small buckets
Five labels for cups or buckets
Small disks or chips
Word list (see below)

What to Do: Label each cup or bucket with one of the five vowels (*a*, *e*, *i*, *o*, or *u*). Place the cups or buckets next to each other on a table or desk.

To begin, say a word and ask a student to identify the vowel sound she hears in the word. For example, "What vowel sound do you hear in the word *shrug*?" From her seat, the student says the vowel and then tosses a chip into the appropriate cup. (Award points for the chips that make it into the cups to boost students' motivation for this activity.) Below are some words to use for this activity.

blend *e*	use *u*	steam *e*
blank *a*	shape *a*	stair *a*
wisp *i*	tried *i*	cute *u*
shop *o*	float *o*	cheese *e*
stub *u*	change *a*	cream *e*
stomp *o*	huge *u*	foam *o*
spill *i*	throat *o*	mail *a*
stem *e*	night *i*	step *e*
crust *u*	kind *i*	soon *u*

Extension Activity

To provide a greater challenge for this activity, you can ask the student to identify whether the vowel sound is "long" or "short" before she tosses the chip into the correct cup.

Short to Long

Objective: Students will change vowel sounds in words from short to long vowels.

Materials: Small ball or beanbag
Word list (see below)

What to Do: This is a wonderful activity for students who are beginning to learn silent *e*. The game begins with the students standing in a circle. Say a word with a short vowel, such as *plan*, and toss a small ball to a student. The student repeats the word, changing the vowel to a long-vowel sound, *plane*. The student then tosses the ball back to you and play continues around the circle.

Some students benefit from visual reinforcement at first, such as writing the target word on the board or a flashcard. Below are some example words for this activity.

can *cane*
rip *ripe*
spit *spite*
back *bake*
met *meet*
stem *steam*
crock *croak*
fill *file*
lid *lied*
slat *slate*
slop *slope*
doll *dole*
flit *flight*

whip *wipe*
rod *road*
step *steep*
cut *cute*
tack *take*
trick *trike*
pill *pile*
past *paste*
mill *mile*
pass *pace*
stack *stake*
slit *slight*
set *seat*

rot *wrote*
lit *light*
us *use*
bet *beat*
lick *like*
hop *hope*
mutt *mute*
bass *base*
fill *file*
tap *tape*
bread *breed*
sweat *sweet*
red *reed*

Extension Activity

Play the game as "Long to Short." Say a long-vowel word and have the student change the vowel to a short-vowel sound.

Vowel Change-Up

Objective: Students will identify the vowel sound in a word and then change the vowel to make a new real word.

Materials: Chalkboard or dry-erase board
Small dry-erase boards or clipboards with slips of scrap paper

What to Do: This is another activity that focuses on manipulating vowel sounds. You can use this game to reinforce both long and short vowels.

Give each student a stimulus word, such as *lick*. The student has to change only the vowel sound to make a new real word, such as *luck* or *lock*. This task can be done orally, with the students taking turns, making new words until all the possibilities are used for each word. You can also record the words on the board, or the students can take turns going to the board to write their own words.

Short Vowels	*Long Vowels*
luck *lick, lack, lock*	while *whale, wheel*
bend *bond, band*	meet *mate, might, moat, mute*
mast *mist, must*	lake *like, leak, luke*
sing *sang, sung, song*	pole *pail, peel, pile*
bank *bunk, bonk*	ride *raid, read, reed, rode, rude*
set *sit, sat*	flight *fleet, float, flute*
bid *bad, bed, bud*	sleet *slight, slate*

Extension Activity

Play "Mind Reading Vowel Change-Up." When you say a word, the students silently write a new word by changing only the vowel. When everyone is ready, show all the possible words. If any of the students' words match, they each earn a point for "reading each other's minds." If no one matches a word, you earn the point.

Drop a Sound

Objective: Students will retain the sequence of sounds, omit a sound in a given word, and repeat the word, omitting the sound.

Materials: Small ball or beanbag
Word list (see below)

What to Do: This is a great activity for students who have trouble retaining the sequence of sounds within a word. The students stand or sit in a circle. Say a word, such as *sit*, and toss a ball or beanbag to one of the students. The student repeats the word, omitting the first sound, *it*.

This game becomes more challenging as the students become more proficient at dropping the initial sounds. The game can progress from consonant-vowel-consonant words, such as *rip*, to words with initial blends. For example, "Drop the second sound of *trip*" yields the word *tip*. Below are some words for this activity.

Drop the Initial Sound	*Drop the Second Sound*
brag *rag*	grease *geese*
trap *rap*	clap *cap*
clap *lap*	stick *sick*
swell *well*	frog *fog*
stick *tick*	drip *dip*
slack *lack*	truck *tuck*
chant *ant*	swing *sing*
shame *aim*	plant *pant*
sleep *leap*	score *sore*
train *rain*	spitting *sitting*
blend *lend*	breach *beach*
switch *witch*	please *peas*
great *rate*	break *bake*

Switch-a-Roo Snake

Objective: Students will practice phoneme substitution to create real words in a word chain task.

Materials: Butcher block paper
Sheets of blank paper
Paste
Marker
Word chain examples
(see page 50)

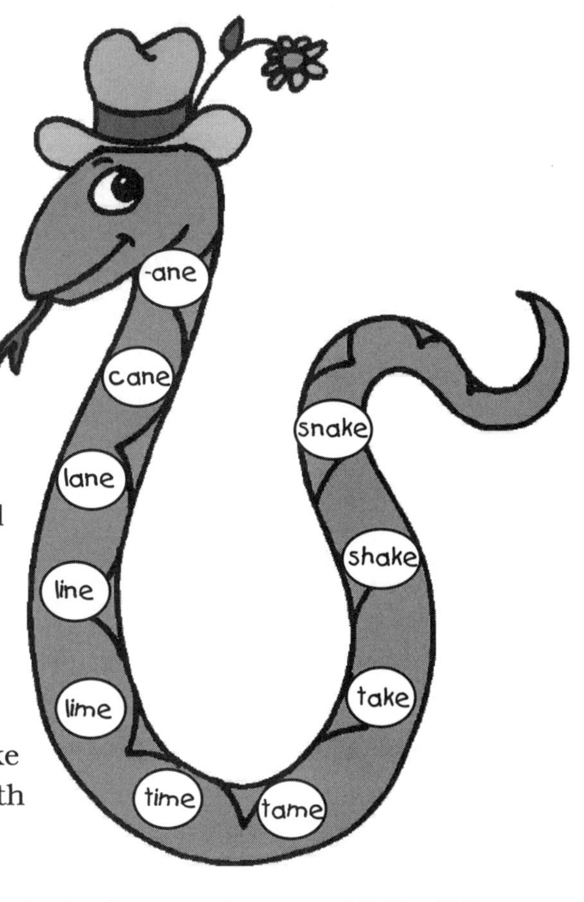

What to Do: Cut out a large shape of a snake (or other large animal) from butcher block paper. Cut eight circles out of blank paper and paste them on the snake's body. Hang the snake on the board or the wall.

-ane
cane
lane
line
lime
time
tame
take
shake
snake

Ask the students to change, delete and/or add sounds to make new words on the snake dots, always ending with the word *snake* on the last dot. For example, begin with *–ane*, then ask the first student to add the "*k*" sound at the beginning (*cane*). Then the second student can change the "*k*" sound to "*l*" (*lane*). Subsequent students can change the long "*a*" sound to long "*i*" (*line*); change the "*n*" sound to "*m*" (*lime*); change the "*l*" sound to "*t*" (*time*); change the long "*i*" sound to long "*a*" (*tame*); change the "*m*" sound to "*k*" (*take*); change the "*t*" *sound* to "*sh*" (*shake*); and, lastly, change the "*sh*" sound to "*sn*" (*snake*). Examples of other word chains are on page 50.

Examples of Word Chains

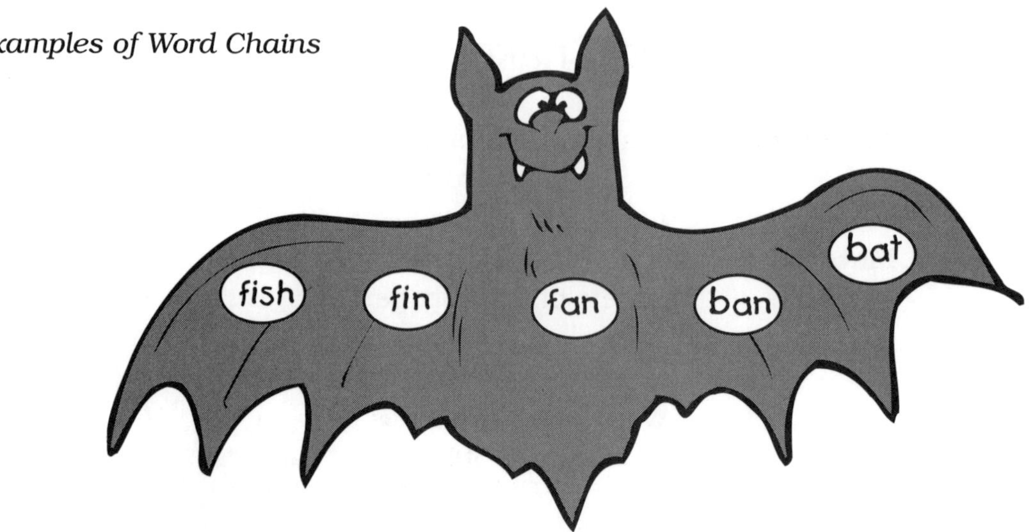

Cut out a paper bat shape and paste five circles on it.

Start with *fish.*
Change the "*sh*" sound to "*n*." *fin*
Change the "*i*" sound to "*a*." *fan*
Change the "*f*" sound to "*b*." *ban*
Change the "*n*" sound to "*t*." *bat*

Cut out a frog shape and paste eight circles on it.

Start with *rat*.
Change the "*r*" sound to "*s*." *sat*
Change the "*a*"" sound to "*i*." *sit*
Change the "*s*"" sound to "*l*." *lit*
Change the "*i*" sound to "*o*." *lot*
Change the "*t*" sound to "*g*." *log*
Change the "*l*" sound to "*f*." *fog*
Add an "*r*" sound after the "*f*." *frog*

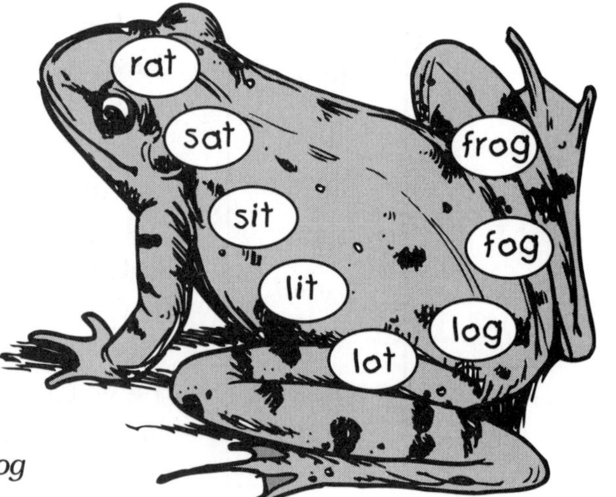

Extension Activity

For a real challenge, have your students create their own animal word transformations.

Word Chains

Objective: Students will manipulate one sound in a word to create a new word.

Materials: Long, narrow piece of paper or sheets of construction paper that are taped together end-to-end

Markers

What to Do: Write a word at the top of the paper, such as *sank*. The first student makes a new word by changing only one sound in your word, such as *sink*, and writes the word below your word. The next student changes another sound in *sink* to make another new word, such as *sing*. This game can go on for days, even weeks, creating a long paper trail that may extend around the entire classroom!

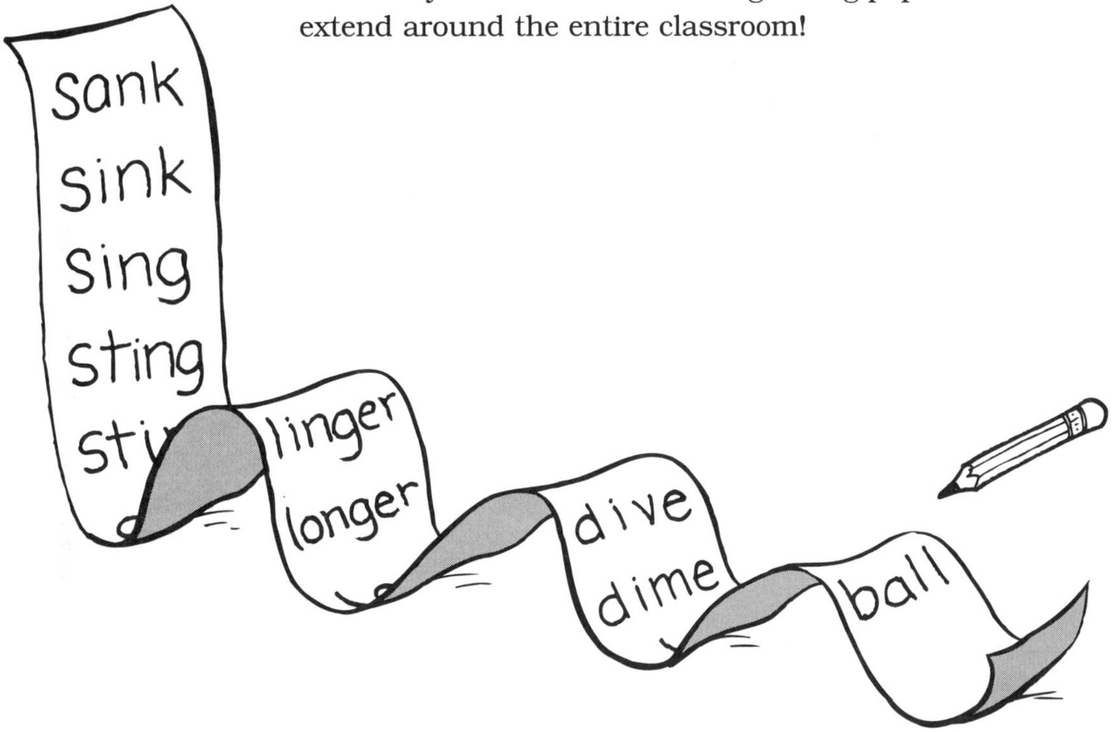

Picture Sort

Objective: Students will categorize or classify words by sounds (initial or final consonants or blends, long vowels, short vowels).

Materials: Pictures or common objects, such as the items below.

candle	pen	die
toy car	tape	scissors
can	tack	coin
card	pad	paper clip
clock	shell	flower

What to Do: Place an assortment of pictures or objects on a table and have the students sort the pictures according to beginning sounds, vowel sounds, and/or ending sounds.

Another way to play is to begin with the assortment of pictures or common objects spread out on a table or on the floor. The students sit in a circle around the objects. Each student takes an even number of pictures or objects and sets them in front of him. When you call out a sound, such as "long *o*," each student who has an object or picture containing that sound holds it up in the air, calling out the word, such as, "I have a boat. The long *o* sound is in the middle of the word." The game continues until all the pictures or objects have been used.

2 Decoding

Many students have difficulty understanding the relationship between speech and print. Developing an understanding of the alphabetic code is necessary for students to acquire word recognition skills. Poor decoding skills slow a student's ability to recognize words, which ultimately affects the student's comprehension of written material. The multisensory activities included in this chapter emphasize decoding and recognizing single and multisyllabic words. In addition, strategies for syllabication and structural analysis of words are presented.

Many of the phonemic awareness activities mentioned in Chapter 1 can be adapted when students are learning to decode words, such as the Extension Activity for Vowel Change-Up, page 47, and Sound Tapping, page 30. See the list below for additional activities from Chapter 1 that can be adapted to teach decoding.

Chapter 1 Activities to Adapt for Decoding

Ring Around the Rhyme, page 23
Word Pattern Categories, page 25
Poetry Completion, page 27
Phoneme Jump, page 38
Vowel Change-Up, page 47
Switch-a-Roo Snake, page 49
Word Chains, page 51

In general, the picture cards used with the rhyming games (pages 18-21) can be substituted with word cards to practice decoding.

Use manipulatives, such as letter tiles, stamping markers, magnets, stamps, and writing with other fun tools to reinforce your instruction. Creating word walls, word banks, word flip books, word boxes, and personal dictionaries are other ways to reinforce decoding skills as well as motivate your students.

Students of all ages love to get their hands dirty. To break up the routine of dictation and drill exercises, try using shaving cream, sand, play dough, etc., to reinforce words for reading and spelling.

Lily Pads

Objective: Students will blend sounds or word parts to make real words.

Materials: Three large pieces of green construction paper
Beanbags or beanbag frogs

What to Do: Cut three lily pads out of green construction paper. On the first lily pad, write the beginning sounds you are working on. These sounds could be single consonants, digraphs, or blends. On the second pad, write vowel sounds—short vowels, vowel teams, or diphthongs. On the last pad, write ending consonants, blends, or digraphs.

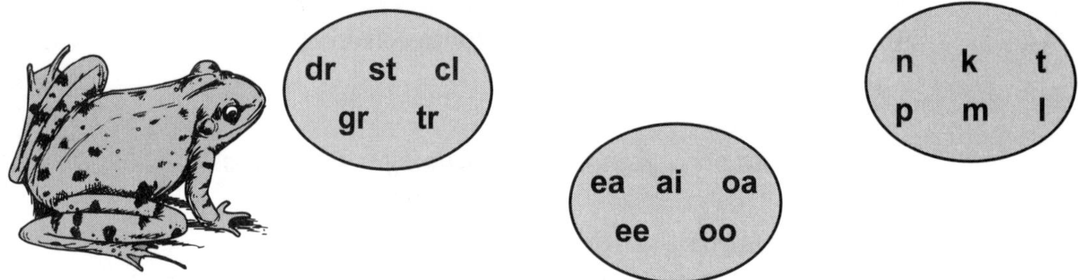

Each student takes a turn tossing a frog onto each pad. Then he combines the sounds that the frog has landed on (or closest to), either orally or on paper, to create a word. If the sounds make a real word (regardless of the spelling), he earns a point. Even though you are not focusing on correct spelling, this is a teachable moment to address the many ways to spell vowel sounds (e.g., *street*, *treat*).

You can pair the students up and have one student record the sounds while the other does the tossing. As the students become more proficient, they may begin to aim for a particular sound to gain a point.

Extension Activity

You can also label the pads with prefixes, roots, and suffixes.

Blends and Ends

Objective: Students will combine onset (the beginning sound or blend) and rime (the vowel and ending sounds—the "pattern") to make real words. For example, in the word *freeze*, the onset is *fr* and the rime is *eeze*.

Materials: Cards with blends and rimes (see pages 56-62)
Two buckets or bags
Paper for recording words

What to Do: Choose the appropriate level of cards for your students.

Level 1	beginning digraphs and short-vowel rimes
Level 2	beginning blends and long-vowel rimes
Level 3	blends and vowel teams
Level 4	blends and diphthongs and other vowel combinations

You can also customize this game by making your own cards. See the list of onsets and rimes on pages 56-57.

Cut up the blends and fold them in half. Put them into the first bucket or bag. Do the same for the rimes, putting them into the other bucket or bag. Each student draws a "blend" and an "end" from the buckets or bags. If the slips combine to make a real word, she writes the word on her paper. The first student to make five (or ten) real words wins.

Extension Activity

Have two students play "Word War" with the words that they make after combining their onset and rimes. If one student has a real word and the other student doesn't, the first student wins that round and collects all the cards. If both students are able to make real words, it's a war. The students then draw again from the bucket or bag to see who has another real word. Whoever can combine a second word wins all the cards again. The game continues until one student can't make a real word.

Choose from these lists to help your students practice with onsets and rimes. Onsets from one level can be combined with rimes from another level. Whenever possible, adapt the activities to the needs of your individual students.

Level 1: Consonants and Digraphs, Short Vowels

Onsets

b	l	r	sh
d	m	s	th
f	n	t	
g	p	w	
h	qu	ch	

Rimes

at	em	ot	
an	eck	op	
am	it	og	*digraphs*
ad	in	ock	ch
ap	ig	ut	tch
ack	id	ud	sh
et	ill	ug	th
en	iss	un	
eg	ick	uck	

Advanced Rimes

amp	eft	ilt	oft	unt
and	ent	int	olt	ust
ant	elf	ist	olf	unk
ast	est	ink	ost	ung
ank	imp	ing	onk	
ang	ind	omp	ong	
end	ift	ond	ump	

Level 2: Blends and Silent *e*

Onsets

br	fr	pr	sp
bl	fl	sc	st
cl	gr	sk	sw
cr	gl	sm	tr
dr	pl	sn	tw

Level 2: Blends and Silent *e* *(continued)*

Rimes

ace	eve	ipe	ope
ade	ibe	ire	ore
age	ide	ite	ove
ake	ice	obe	ume
ale	ife	ode	une
ame	ike	oke	use
ane	ile	ole	ute
ape	ime	ome	
ate	ine	one	

Level 3: Blends and Vowel Teams

Onsets

br	dr	gl	scr	sp	str
bl	fr	pl	sk	spr	sw
cl	fl	pr	sm	squ	tr
cr	gr	sc	sn	st	tw

Rimes

aid	eef	eeze	eat	oan
ail	eek	ead	eave	oap
ain	eel	eak	ew	oar
air	eem	eal	oad	oat
ait	een	eam	oaf	oast
aw	eep	ean	oak	oave
ay	eer	ear	oal	
eed	eet	ease	oam	

Level 4: Blends and Diphthongs/Other Vowel Combinations

Onsets

br	dr	gl	scr	sp	str
bl	fr	pl	sk	spr	sw
cl	fl	pr	sm	squ	tr
cr	gr	sc	sn	st	tw

Rimes

aw	igh	oise	oor	out	own
awl	ight	ood	oud	ouse	oy
ew	oil	ook	ound	ow	ue
eud	oin	oom	oul	owd	uise
eul	oist	oove	our	owl	y

Copy this page. Cut the boxes apart to use for word-building activities.

Level 1, Beginning: Digraphs (onsets)

ch	sh	th
wh	sh	wh
ch	sh	th
ch	sh	th

Level 1, Beginning: Ends (rimes)

op	at	ick
ock	in	ing
mp	unk	en
ut	ug	ink

Copy this page. Cut the boxes apart to use for word-building activities.

Level 1, Advanced: Digraphs (onsets)

ch	sh	th
wh	sh	wh
ch	sh	th
ch	sh	th

Level 1, Advanced: Ends (rimes)
These can also be combined with Level 2 blends.

ing	ink	unk
amp	elf	est
ump	ank	imp

Copy this page. Cut the boxes apart to use for word-building activities.

Level 2: Blends (onsets)

cl	sl	bl
br	cr	tr
st	sp	sk
sn	sw	tw

Level 2 Ends (rimes—silent e*)*

ite	ale	oke
ade	ane	ate
ide	ine	une
ude	one	ole

Copy this page. Cut the boxes apart to use for word-building activities.

Level 3: Blends (onsets)

cl	sl	bl
br	cr	tr
st	sp	sl
sn	sw	gr

Level 3 Ends (rimes—vowel combinations)

ight	ail	oak
ay	ain	eat
eep	air	eer
eak	ease	eeze

Copy this page. Cut the boxes apart to use for word-building activities.

Level 4: Blends (onsets)

cl	sl	bl
br	cr	tr
st	sp	sk
sn	sw	gr

Level 4 Ends (rimes)

ow (as in *cow*)	ow (long *o*)	own
y (long *i*)	out	uise
awl	ew	ue
oil	ouse	ound

Clip It

Objective: Students will combine onsets and rimes to make real words.

Materials: Index cards with rimes printed on them
Clothespins with blends printed on them
Paper and pens/pencils for students to record words
List of onsets and rimes (choose from pages 56-57)

What to Do: Give each student an index card and several clothespins. The students match the blends on the clothespins with the rimes on the index cards to make real words. (To individualize, create cards and clothespins that focus on the patterns a student is studying.) Students record their words on paper, trying to make as many words as they can within a time limit. When the time is up (two minutes is usually enough time), the student with the most words recorded wins.

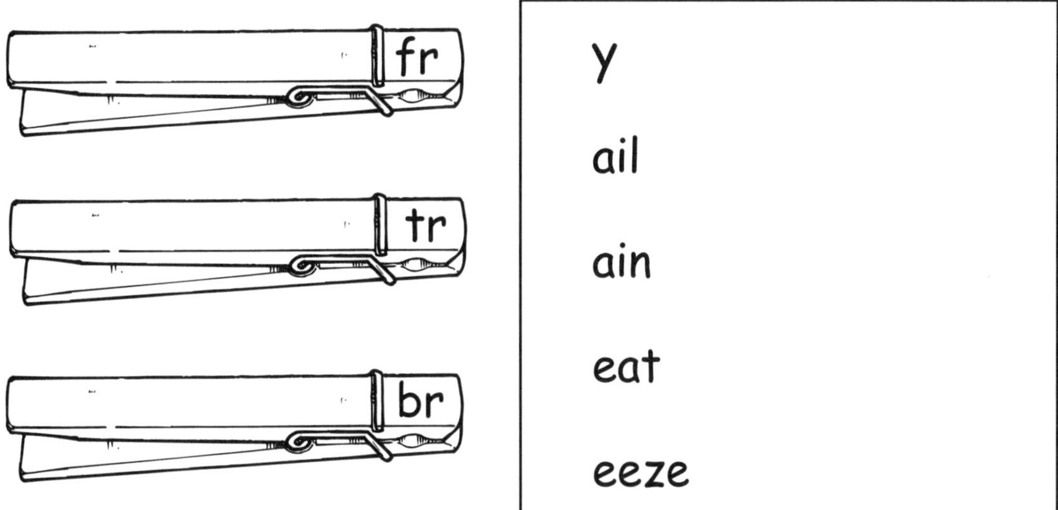

Extension Activity

Give all students the same clothespin onsets and rimes on cards. Have each student read the words generated aloud. If one student's word matches another student's word, both students cross out the word on their cards. Assign points for any remaining words.

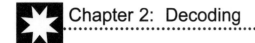

Word Webs

Objective: Students will combine onsets and rimes to make real words.

Materials: Word webs (see examples below and on pages 65-66)

What to Do: Give each student a web that includes a word pattern in the middle of the web and beginning consonants, digraphs, or blends as connecting extensions of the web. Students blend a beginning sound (onset) and the target pattern (rime) to read each word. You can do this activity orally or in writing.

Level 1 Word Webs

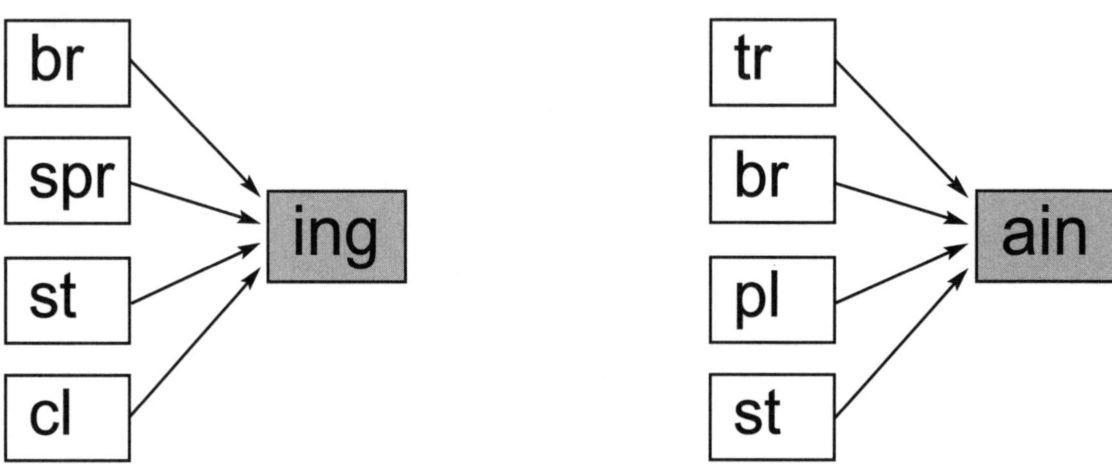

Extension Activity

To make the webs more challenging, have your students think of as many words as they can that contain the target pattern. The students can try to make their word webs as big as they can.

Level 2 Word Webs

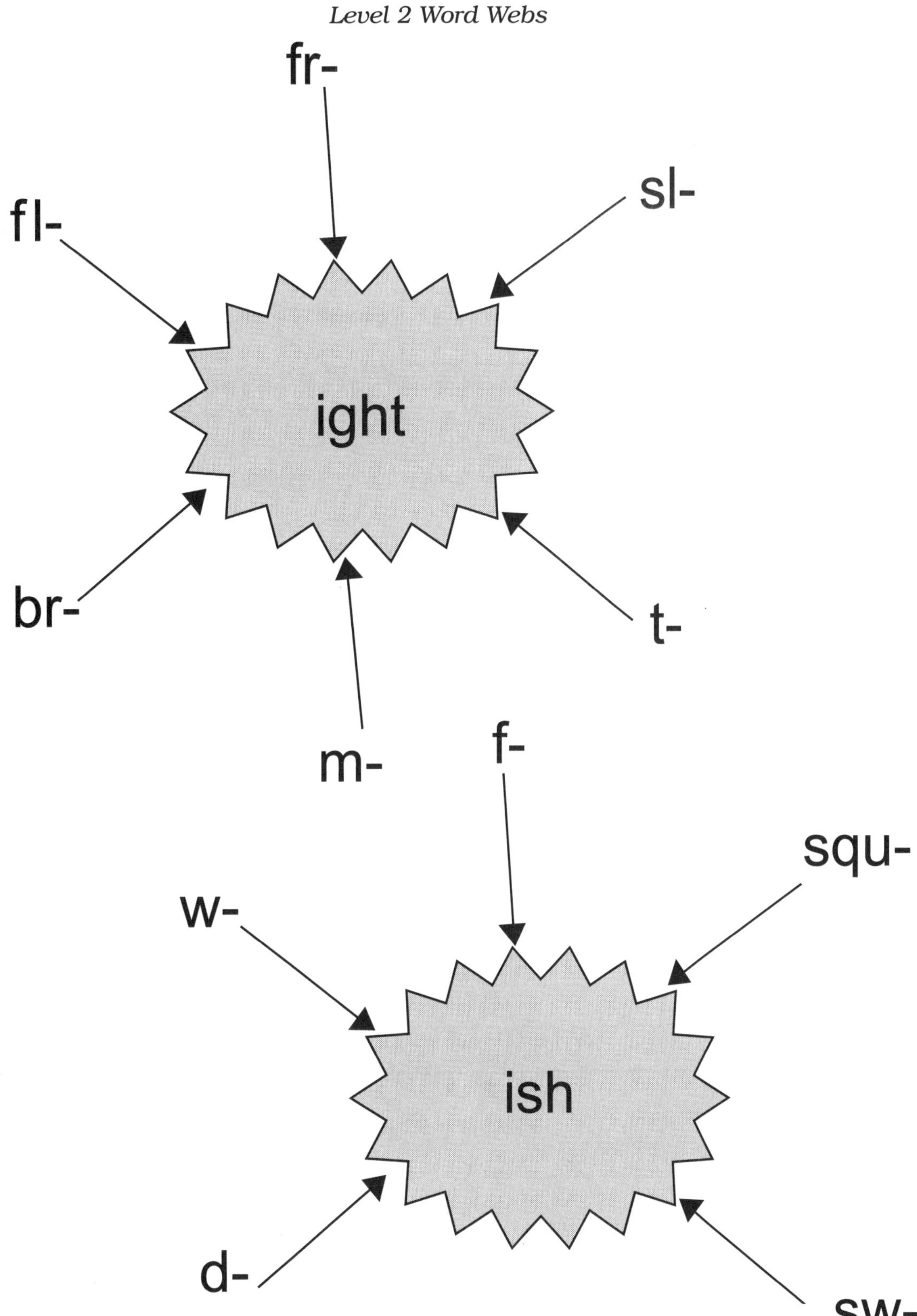

Word Web Patterns

Level 1

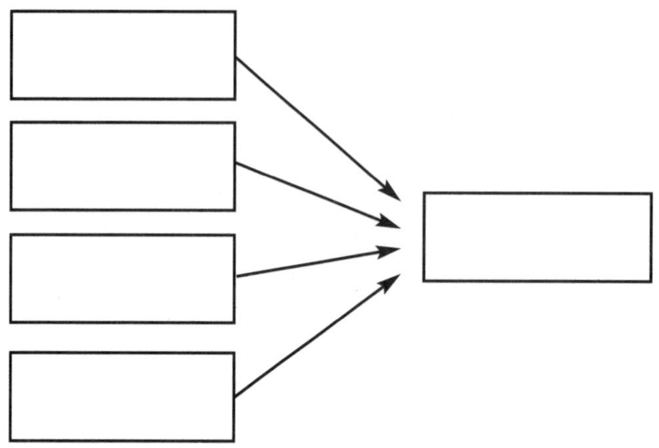

Level 2

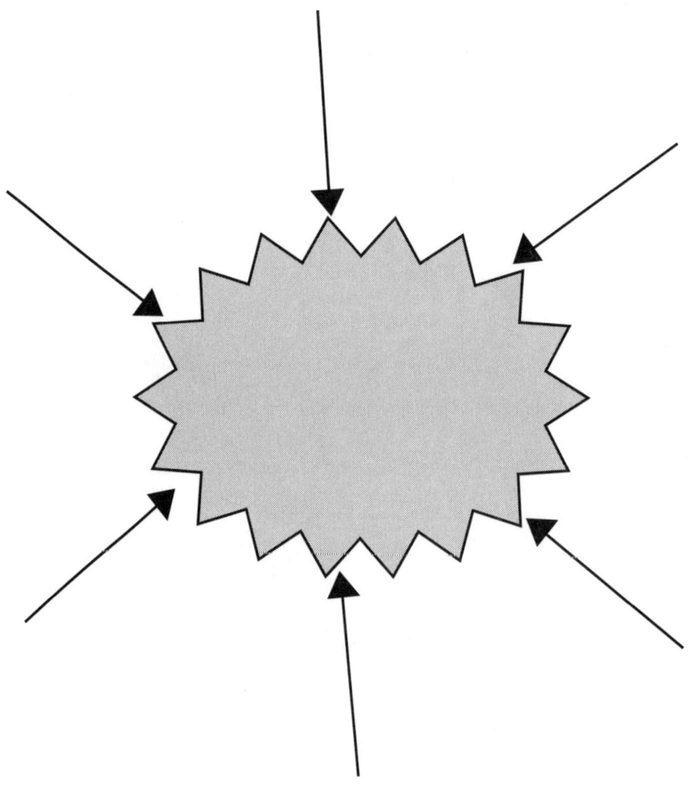

Highlighter Detectives

Objective: Students will recognize sounds, patterns, letter combinations, or words within text.

Materials: Word lists, stories, or articles
Highlighters
Magnifying glass (optional)

What to Do: Give each student a word list (or article, story, etc.) and a highlighter. Ask each student to search his story for a target sound, pattern, or word and highlight every occurrence. Some students become really motivated to search for words if you give them a magnifying glass to search through the text. Let them know that they are "detectives" looking for the sounds or words. An example passage is below; the target word is *serum.*

History of the Iditarod

In 1925, an epidemic of a terrible disease, diphtheria (diff-theer-ee-uh), hit the small town of Nome, Alaska. A **serum** was needed, but was in short supply. Airplanes in the area were grounded because of bad weather. The **serum** had to be rushed from Nenana to Nome or many people would die. Nenana was 675 miles from Nome. Dog sled teams took the **serum** to Nome. It took the sled teams just 127 hours to get the **serum** to Nome.

The Iditarod is run every year to honor and remember that historic run in 1925. The race begins in Anchorage during the first weekend in March. The first race took place in 1973, and the finish time was about 20 days. Now the finish times have dropped to under ten days!

Extension Activity

Using more sophisticated text may be appropriate for some students. Have them search and highlight high-frequency words.

Word Sort

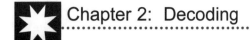

Objective: Students will sort words by vowel sounds.

Materials: Five paper plates, each labeled with a vowel
Ten large craft sticks per set (see lists below and on page 69)

What to Do: Spread the five paper plates on the floor. On each craft stick, write a word that contains a long-vowel sound. Make sure that you include many different spellings for the same sound. For example, here are some words for the long *a* sound: *explain, staying, baker, grateful.* When you say "Go!," the students race to sort their words by long-vowel sounds by putting each word on the appropriate plate. The first player to sort all of her words wins the game.

Level 1 Word Sets (single-syllable words, short vowels)

Set 1		***Set 2***	
trash	rang	match	land
belt	send	left	bent
lint	swing	wind	fist
shop	chomp	stomp	pond
trust	hung	bunk	dump

Set 3		***Set 4***	
bath	fang	raft	smash
felt	deck	sled	spend
grill	limp	trip	bring
chop	lock	golf	plot
fuss	dunk	stuff	rush

Level 2 Word Sets *(single-syllable words, long vowels)*

Set 1		***Set 2***	
train	brave	braid	grade
eve	steam	clean	steep
pile	flight	slime	right
stone	roam	stove	road
fuse	cute	use	mute

Level 2 Word Sets *(continued)*

Set 3

chain	crane
dream	wheel
thigh	pride
drove	coat
flute	cube

Set 4

pail	shame
read	feel
night	time
cone	toast
tube	fuse

Level 3 Word Sets *(two-syllable words, long vowels)*

Set 1

explain	basement
hungry	weakness
lighter	trying
sofa	solo
confuse	excuse

Set 2

neighbor	statement
windy	cheerful
lightning	advice
broken	untold
acute	amuse

Set 3

weight	training
agree	fancy
midnight	flying
hotel	snowfall
exclude	accuse

Set 4

playful	table
concrete	increase
quiet	shyness
smoking	poet
untrue	useful

Set 5

stranger	staple
athlete	needle
cider	license
choking	blowing
miscue	rhubarb

Set 6

pages	able
steeple	complete
spider	uptight
floating	spoken
cutest	volume

Extension Activity

You can create your own sets of words based on the patterns that your students have learned. You can also have groups of students create appropriate lists.

Die-Gories

Objective: Students will use a die and categories to review words being studied for decoding and/or spelling.

Materials: Die
Word list (see below)
Die-Gories chart (page 71)

What to Do: Each student will roll a die. Then you will ask the student to answer a question about the words being studied, based on the number the student rolled. Below are sample questions for each of the categories on the Die-Gories chart.

To make this game more active, have the student take a shot with a basketball and hoop if he answers a question correctly. The students can also play for points, earning one point for each correct answer.

Number Rolled	*Category*	*Sample Question*
6	Spelling	Spell the word *sauce*.
5	Phonemes/ Syllables	How many sounds are in the word *city*?
4	Sentence	Use *accept* in a sentence.
3	Rhyme	What word rhymes with *chance*?
2	Choice	(Student selects a category.)
1	Change It	Change the first syllable in *conceive* to the syllable *re-*. What is the new word?

Die-Gories

Number	Category
6	Spelling
5	Phonemes/Syllables
4	Sentence
3	Rhyme
2	Choice
1	Change It

Word Bingo

Objective: Students will identify and decode words being studied.

Materials: One copy of the Word Bingo form (page 73) per student
Chips
Word lists

What to Do: Copy one blank Bingo board for each player. Write the sounds or words being studied in the Bingo squares (see the examples below), changing the location of the sounds or words on each board. Give each player a Bingo card and some chips.

Call out one of the sounds or words in the set. Students listen and look for the sound or word on their boards. When they find it, they cover it with a chip. The first player to cover five sounds or words in a row (vertically, horizontally, or diagonally) wins the game. You can also play until the whole Bingo board is covered (a "Blackout").

Word Bingo				
cut	dog	fit	pup	bed
rag	ten	lip	cut	hot
hum	tap	**FREE**	win	set
hem	wag	leg	but	rod
not	tan	rim	run	men

Word Bingo				
crease	tooth	spoil	while	sprain
cage	crown	light	spruce	throat
huge	great	**FREE**	mild	sweet
broil	noise	speak	fry	road
note	taste	choose	paste	mean

Word Bingo

		FREE		

Word Path

Objective: Students will practice reading words they are studying.

Materials: 13 sheets of various colors of construction paper
25 two-inch squares of the same colors of construction paper
Small bag or bucket

What to Do: This activity is played much like the classic board game Candy Land. Cut the whole sheets of construction paper in half (8½" x 5½"). Write each word that needs to be reviewed on a separate piece of construction paper.

Place the words in a path starting in the classroom and continuing out the door, into the hallway, as far as you can go!

Each student takes a turn picking a small colored paper square from a bag or bucket. Starting at the beginning of the path, a student reads the words on each card until the student gets to the color on the path that matches the square she pulled from the bag or bucket. The number of words the student has to read will be random—she may draw a slip with a color five steps away or two steps away. Either way, she must read all the words along the way. For example, if she pulls a green square from the bag or bucket, she advances to the nearest green spot on the floor, reading each word along the way.

Extension Activity

Add five "golden cards" to the pile of colored cards. When a student pulls a golden card, ask her a bonus question, such as one of the examples below.

Give me three words that rhyme with the word you're standing on.

Tell me how many sounds are in the word you're standing on.

Use the word in a sentence.

Tell me three words that have the same vowel sound as your word.

If the student answers correctly, she may move ahead three spaces.

Syllabication

Lots of techniques can be used to reinforce syllable counting, such as clapping, jumping, using the whole arm to tap out segments, and using a xylophone or a drum. But beware! Students may become easily confused if you use the same movement or a similar movement as you used when counting phonemes. Make sure your techniques are clearly different.

Once your students become proficient with single syllables, you can combine syllables to make multisyllabic words. However, you should introduce multisyllabic consonant-vowel-consonant compound words at the very beginning stages of decoding, such as *sunset, tidbit,* and *backpack.* This early introduction will motivate your students as they apply their decoding skills to read "bigger" words.

Teaching students how to divide words into syllables can be tedious. Using a jazzy hook like "Zeus's lightning bolts" (or Harry Potter's scar) can really make a difference, as in the examples below. The Syllable Bolts form on the next page may help your students practice syllabication by writing words in syllables and using visual memory to form an image of the way the words are divided. Example multisyllabic words are listed on pages 77-78.

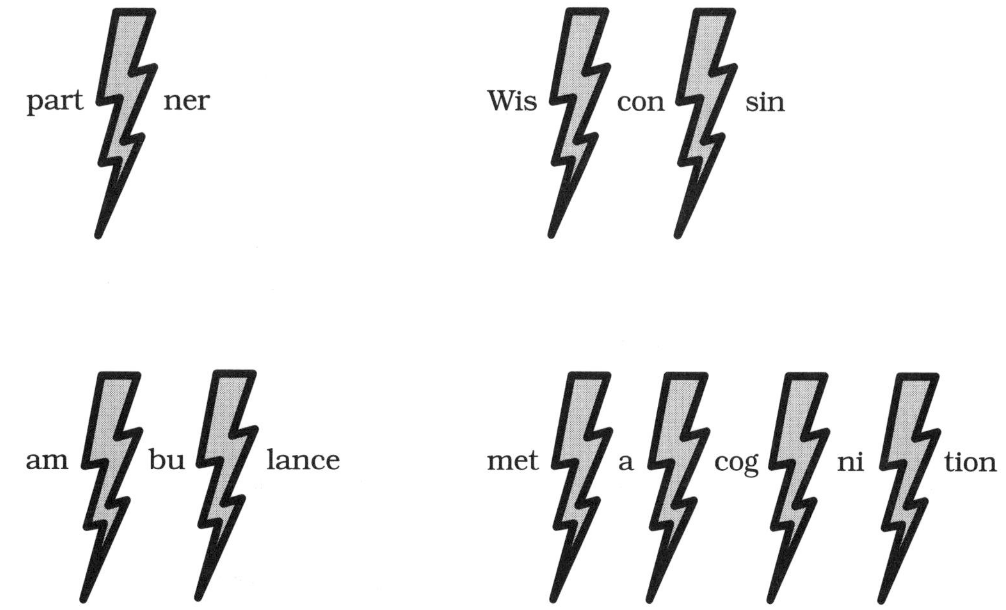

Syllable Bolts

Use the patterns on this page to divide words into syllables.

2-syllable words ________ ________

3-syllable words ________ ________ ________

4-syllable words ________ ________ ________ ________

5-syllable words ________ ________ ________ ________ ________

Multisyllabic Words

Two-Syllable Compound Words

in • to	cow • boy	rain • coat	may • be
lunch • box	oat • meal	sail • boat	back • pack

Two-Syllable Words

trum • pet	mim • ic	sta • ble	dis • tant
ti • tle	per • sist	un • der	in • vite
ab • sent	mu • sic	ex • pire	per • son
gig • gle	tat • tle	fe • ver	wag • on
drag • on	di • et	qui • et	ru • in
sub • way	sham • poo	stu • dent	ho • tel
com • ic	ran • dom	prob • lem	fa • ble
puz • zle	pep • per	com • et	de • pend
sus • pect	sup • pose	ex • pert	sta • ple
mo • ment	hun • dred	stee • ple	ex • claim
flu • id	re • act	re • ceive	poi • son
pew • ter	um • pire	ba • con	in • spire
in • side	be • fore	lem • on	per • fume
in • clude	ex • pand	po • et	o • ver
ex • treme	en • ter	con • vince	e • lect
sev • en	lo • cate	cre • ate	flu • ent
tri • umph	neigh • bor	oys • ter	se • cret

Three-Syllable Words

e • quip • ment	ad • vi • sor	re • ac • tion	wil • der • ness
so • lo • ist	hyp • no • tize	ro • man • tic	re • fresh • ment
grad • u • ate	rep • re • sent	tux • e • do	mi • cro • scope
tur • pen • tine	mem • o • rize	dis • a • ble	in • flu • ence
vi • o • lin	pi • o • neer	av • e • nue	neigh • bor • hood
con • tin • ue	as • sem • ble	en • ter • tain	dif • fer • ent
im • por • tant	mir • a • cle	spec • ta • tor	in • spec • tor
va • ca • tion	ex • am • ple	mu • se • um	ro • de • o
vi • o • lence	in • ter • view	At • lan • tic	op • er • ate
in • tro • duce	in • ter • rupt	il • lus • trate	in • for • mal
vi • o • lent	re • gard • less	pow • er • less	un • der • stand

Four-Syllable Words

in • for • ma • tion	in • vi • ta • tion
con • stel • la • tion	mon • u • men • tal
rep • u • ta • tion	il • lus • tra • tion
in • tro • duc •tion	u • ni • ver • sal

Five-Syllable Words

com • mu • ni • ca • tion	un • hes • i • tat • ing
u • ni • fi • ca • tion	un • for • get • ta • ble
for • ti • fi • ca • tion	il • lu • mi • na • tion

Syllable Match-Up

Objective: Students will combine syllables to make real words.

Materials: Index cards
Envelopes to store sets of syllables
Syllable list (see pages 80-81)

What to Do: Cut the index cards into thirds. Write one syllable on each small card. As a warmup for this activity, have the students sort the syllables by type onto a paper chart (see chart below). Give the student a set of three syllables and see if she can use two of the three syllables to make a real word, such as *ar, dis, gue = argue*). This process will reinforce decoding certain syllable types. You can expand this activity to three-syllable words as well, requiring the students to use all three syllables to create a three-syllable word, such as *cov, er, dis = discover.*

closed	**open**	**silent *e***
dis		
vowel team	***r*-controlled**	**consonant *-le***
gue	ar	

The lists on the following page include all syllable types. Tailor the sets of syllables to the individual student's level. Select types you have already taught your students. For example, if some students have not yet learned vowel combination syllables or consonant *-le* syllables, leave those syllable types out of the game.

Syllable List

Syllable Sets for "Two of Three" Game (the first two syllables make the word)

trum • pet • ment

mim • ic • out

sta • ble • tion

dis • tant • me

ti • tle • ble

per • sist • gle

un • der • ble

in • vite • ful

ab • sent • ser

mu • sic • ver

ex • pire • tire

per • son • fer

gig • gle • ble

tat • tle • fle

fe • ver • dred

wag • on • der

drag • on • mer

di • et • robe

qui • et • ler

ru • in • lert

sub • way • bay

sham • poo • lam

ho • tel • per

com • ic • pre

ran • dom • kin

prob • lem • or

fa • ble • ter

puz • zle • num

pep • per • ist

com • et • fer

de • pend • ic

sus • pect • ile

sup • pose • vil

ex • pert • try

sta • ple • tle

mo • ment • en

hun • dred • mer

stee • ple • dle

ex • claim • flame

flu • id • ber

re • act • mile

re • ceive • lance

poi • son • lon

pew • ter • few

ba • con • er

in • spire • tion

in • side • ar

be • fore • com

lem • on • ir

per • fume • ist

in • clude • vit

ex • pand • ize

po • et • nid

o • ver • ber

ex • treme • em

en • ter • ver

con • vince • dant

e • lect • zen

sev • en • let

lo • cate • mate

cre • ate • ver

flu • ent • mer

tri • umph • ence

neigh • bor • tor

oys • ter • per

se • cret • ber

Syllable Sets for "Three of Three" Game (all three syllables make the word)

e • quip • ment	re • fresh • ment	in • flu • ence
ad • vi • sor	grad • u • ate	vi • o • lin
wil • der • ness	mi • cro • scope	pi • o • neer
re • ac • tion	tux • e • do	mu • se • um
so • lo • ist	rep • re • sent	ro • de • o
hyp • no • tize	tur • pen • tine	vi • o • lence
ro • man • tic	per • ma • nent	neigh • bor • hood
dis • a • ble	ex • am • ple	av • e • nue
con • tin • ue	as • sem • ble	en • ter • tain
dif • fer • ent	im • por • tant	mir • a • cle
spec • ta • tor	in • spec • tor	in • ter • view
At • lan • tic	op • er • ate	in • tro • duce
in • ter • rupt	il • lus • trate	in • for • mal
vi • o • lent	re • gard • less	pow • er • less

Newt Roots

Objective: Students will gain a better understanding of structural analysis, prefixes, base words, and suffixes.

Materials: Paper "newts" cut into heads, bodies, and tails (see page 83)
List of base words, prefixes, and suffixes (see below)

What to Do: This is a great way to illustrate structural analysis concretely. The newt's body is the root/base word, the head is the prefix, and the tail is the suffix. It works like a puzzle. The students add prefixes and suffixes to the root words to create new, real words. Write base words and affixes on appropriate newt parts. Give each student two or three newt pieces to form words and tape the pieces of the word together. Have each student record his words on paper and then compare his list with his classmates' lists. This activity works well for small groups of two or three students.

Prefixes	*Base Words*	*Suffixes*
un-	play	-ful
re-	plant	-ness
pre-	happy	-less
dis-	health	-y
mis-	teach	-er
ex-	cold	-ist
bi-	direct	-ment
tri-	friend	-ship
trans-	view	-ing
ab-	normal	-tion
de-	port	-able
per-	capable	-ity
dia-	meter	-ist
pro-	able	-sion
multi-	assist	-ance
sub-	hope	-dom
non-	simple	-ify
extra-	home	-ly
semi-	rain	-en

Copy these newt shapes, one set per word for the Newt Roots activity, page 82.

Word Parts

Objective: Students will identify meanings of prefixes, suffixes, and roots, and provide examples of each.

Materials: Word parts list (see page 82)
Word Parts Game sheet (page 85)
Die

What to Do: After spending some time on word study, generate lists of:

a. prefixes and words that contain those prefixes
b. roots and words that contain those roots

Then post these word lists in the classroom.

Post the Word Parts Game sheet where everyone can see it. Have your students take turns rolling the die. Ask the student a question based on the number the student rolled. Below are sample questions for each number on the die.

Number Rolled	*Task*	*Sample Question*
6	Prefix Example	Tell me a word that has the prefix *in-*.
5	Root Example	Tell me a word that has the root *port*.
4	Sentence	Use the word *transport* in a sentence.
3	Choice	(Student selects a task.)
2	Prefix Meaning	What does the prefix *sub-* mean?
1	Root Meaning	What does the root *port* mean?

Word Parts

Number	Task
6	Prefix Example
5	Root Example
4	Sentence
3	Choice
2	Prefix Meaning
1	Root Meaning

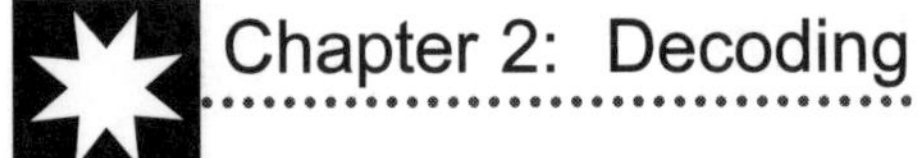

Bubblegum Machine

Objective: Students will enhance their understanding of structural analysis by combining prefixes or suffixes with base words to create new words.

Materials: Bubblegum machine made out of construction paper
Circles of construction paper to be gumballs
Student copies of Bubblegum Machine (page 87, optional)
Small cards to label with target prefixes and suffixes
List of prefixes and suffixes (see below)

What to Do: You can use this activity to practice using prefixes or suffixes. The students fill in the gumballs, using the target prefix or suffix from the base of the machine. If a student has difficulty generating words, the dictionary becomes a great resource. This is a great group activity; the students can work in pairs to fill up the bubblegum machine. You can also give students individual copies of Bubblegum Machine, page 87.

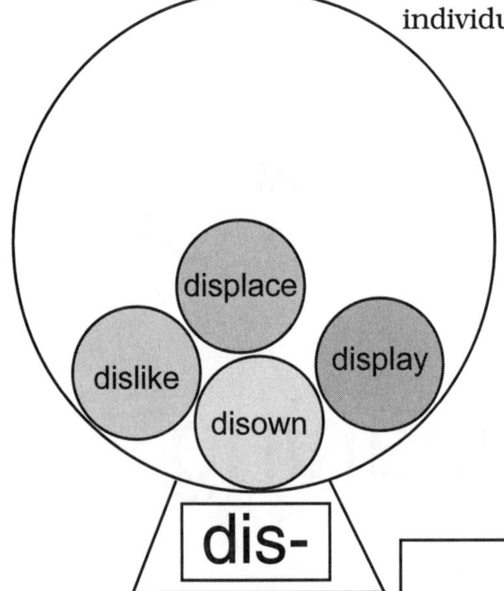

Prefixes	*Suffixes*
un-	-ful
re-	-ness
pre-	-less
dis-	-y
mis-	-er
ex-	-ist
bi-	-ment
tri-	-ship
trans-	-ing
in-	-ly

Extension Activity

Enrich this activity by including base words in addition to prefixes and suffixes. Try the words below.

play	plant	happy	health	view
teach	cold	direct	friend	place

Bubblegum Machine

Follow your teacher's directions to fill in this bubblegum machine.

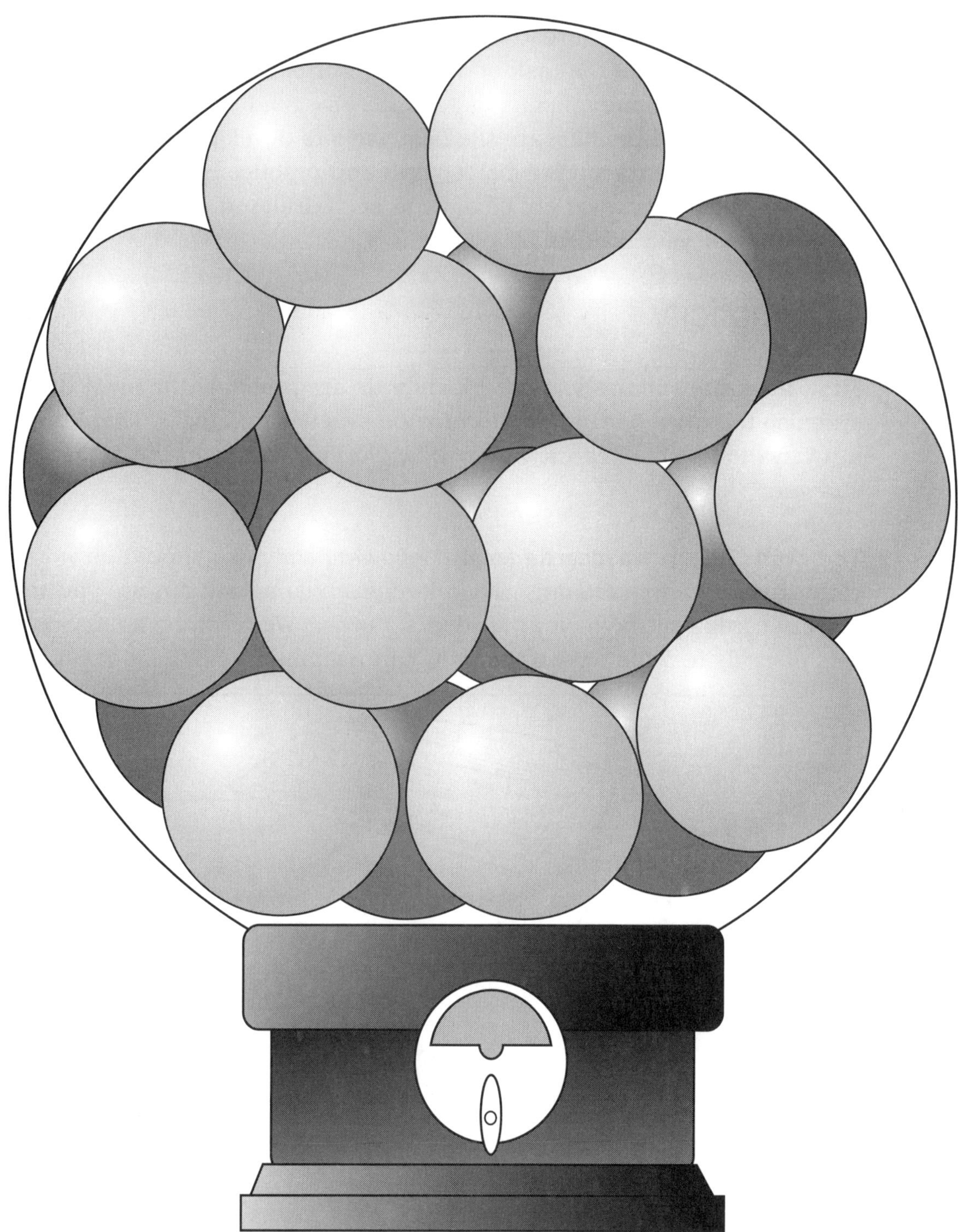

3 Automaticity and Fluency

Automaticity and fluency are the end goals for decoding instruction. In order for students to understand what they read, they need to be able to recognize words automatically and read text fluently. **Automaticity** means not needing to devote attention to the task of decoding words while reading (Johns and Lenski 1997). **Fluency** means fast, expressive reading (Cunningham 2000). Drill and repeated practice are the best ways to develop automaticity and fluency, yet students often consider drill and practice mundane. The activities in this chapter offer a variety of ways to keep drill and practice both fun and motivating for your students.

Automaticity

First, a note about flashcards. Flashcards are probably the most traditional, and also the most boring, way to provide practice and drill. There are lots of fun ways to use flashcards, however, as you will see from the activities in this chapter.

The words on the flashcards for the following activities should be words that your students are practicing. Therefore, each game will require you to create a set of cards specific to your students' needs. We recommend saving your sets of cards in a file box so that you can use and reuse them easily.

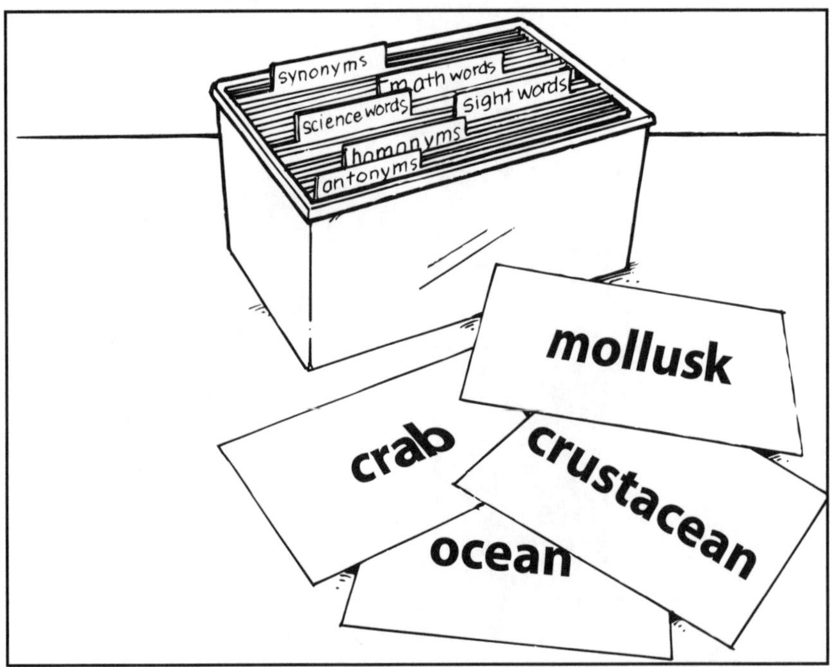

Quick Flash

Objective: Students will increase the speed with which they read instructed words.

Materials: Index cards with instructed words printed on the cards

What to Do: Flash the student a word card and quickly place the card back down on the table. The student says each word as you flash through the stack of cards. If the student doesn't recognize a word or reads a word incorrectly, he can ask to see the word again by saying "Quick Flash!" The goal is to get through the pile of words as fast as he can without requesting a "Quick Flash."

Go Fish

Objective: Students will increase the speed with which they read instructed words.

Materials: Index cards with target words printed on one side (two cards for each word)

What to Do: Play this game just like the traditional card game, only these cards have words on them. It is best to play with a deck of at least 30 cards (two each of 15 words). Deal five cards to each player. The object of the game is to collect the most pairs of matching words.

One player begins by asking another player if she has a word that the player possesses already, such as, "Jill, do you have the word *some*?" If that player has the word, she relinquishes the card. The asking player takes the pair and puts the cards faceup on the table. If the other player does not have the card, she says, "Go Fish," and the asking player draws a card from the pile. When all the cards are used, the player who has the most pairs wins the game.

Extension Activity

In addition to looking for matching words, the students can also look for words that rhyme, have similar vowel sounds, have beginning or ending blends that match, etc.

This game can also be played with synonyms, antonyms, or homonym pairs. Once a student collects a pair, she must use the words correctly in a sentence in order to keep the pair. If not, the cards go back in the drawing pile.

Memory

Objective: Students will increase the speed with which they read instructed words.

Materials: Index cards with instructed words printed on them (two cards per word)

What to Do: Shuffle the word cards and put them facedown on a table. The students take turns turning over two cards at a time, trying to uncover matching words. Each time a student turns over a card, he must say the word quickly, without hesitation, and repeat the word when he turns the card back over again. Students keep each pair they identify and read correctly. The winner is the student with the most pairs of cards when all the cards have been uncovered.

Extension Activity

In addition to looking for matching words, students can also look for words that rhyme, have similar vowel sounds, have beginning or ending blends that match, etc. This game can also be played with homonym pairs (see list below). Once a student collects a pair, he must use the words correctly in a sentence in order to keep the pair. If not, the cards go back in the pile.

Homonyms

ate	eight	be	bee
bare	bear	berry	bury
blew	blue	cell	sell
chews	choose	dear	deer
eye	I	fair	fare
hear	here	know	no
meat	meet	son	sun
wear	where	their	there
buy	by	cent	scent

Word Hunt

Objective: Students will increase the speed with which they read instructed words.

Materials: 10-20 index cards with target words printed on them

What to Do: Ask the students to put their heads down or wait outside the classroom while you hide the cards around the room. The students enter the room and immediately begin hunting for the words, reading each word aloud before looking for the next card. Every time a student finds another word, he reads all the words in his hand before looking for the next word. When all the words have been collected, the student with the most words wins.

Extension Activity

You can also have the students categorize the words according to vowel sounds, ending sounds, or beginning sounds. In addition, you can have the students alphabetize their collected words.

Roll 'em and Read 'em

Objective: Students will increase the speed with which they read instructed words.

Materials: die
50 or more index cards with target words printed on them

What to Do: Place a stack of cards in the middle of a group of students. (If you are working with a larger group, you may want to split the students into two smaller groups.)

Each student takes a turn rolling the die and then draws that number of cards from the pile. She reads the cards quickly, without hesitation, and then places the cards in her pile.

Each time a student has a turn, she must read the words in her pile before rolling the die.

Play continues until all the cards have been read. The last player has to roll the exact number to get the remaining cards.

While each student waits for her next turn, she can do one or more of the tasks below with the word cards she holds.

- ✓ Record the words on paper.
- ✓ Categorize the words by blend, vowel sounds, etc.
- ✓ Organize the word cards in alphabetical order.
- ✓ Divide the words into syllables.
- ✓ Write a sentence using each of the words.

Minute Mastery

Objective: Students will increase the speed with which they read instructed words.

Materials: 50 or more index cards with target words printed on them
Minute timer

What to Do: We have found that groups of three to five students work best for this activity. Arrange the students in a circle. Then divide the cards among them. When the timer begins, each student takes a turn reading the top card of his pile. After he reads a word, he drops the word into a pile or box in the center of the circle.

The goal is to see how many words the group can read before the minute is up. As a group, they want to increase the number of words they read in a minute. If the group is too large, split the group into smaller groups.

Rats! (for Words)

Objective: Students will increase the speed with which they read instructed words.

Materials: Small bucket, bowl, or bag

For each player, five to six small slips of paper with words printed on them (e.g., 50-60 word slips for ten students)

Five to ten slips of paper with the word *Rats!* printed on them (or copy the template below)

What to Do: Fold all the slips of paper and place them into the bucket, bowl, or bag. Each student takes a turn pulling the slips of paper and reading the words. If she draws a *Rats!*, she must read all the slips she has acquired, then put them back into the bucket, bowl, or bag. The first player to collect five word slips wins.

I Have ____. Who Has ____?

Objective: Students will increase the speed with which they read instructed words.

Materials: Copies of page 97 (enough for each player to have at least four cards)

What to Do: Shuffle the cards and deal an even number to each student. Each card says "I have (target word)" at the top and "Who has (target word)" at the bottom (see examples below). For the first card below, the player would say, "I have *spend.* Who has *spent*?" The player who has *spent* at the top of a card goes next—"I have *spent.* Who has *spot*?" and so on. The cards are turned over as they're read.

Extension Activity

This game can be played as a team, while you time the "round" to see how long it takes to complete. The game can also be played to see who turns over all of his cards first.

I have ____. spend Who has ____? blend	I have ____. blend Who has ____? rent	I have ____. rent Who has ____? spent	I have ____. spent Who has ____? hint
I have ____. hint Who has ____? grand	I have ____. grand Who has ____? grunt	I have ____. grunt Who has ____? grin	I have ____. grin Who has ____? think

Copy this page and cut the cards apart for "I Have ____. Who Has ____?," page 96. Write the target words on each card.

I have ____. Who has ____?	I have ____. Who has ____?	I have ____. Who has ____?
I have ____. Who has ____?	I have ____. Who has ____?	I have ____. Who has ____?
I have ____. Who has ____?	I have ____. Who has ____?	I have ____. Who has ____?

Bingo

Objective: Students will increase the speed with which they read instructed words.

Materials: One Bingo grid (page 73) per player
List of words to call for Bingo game
Small plastic disks, chips, or coins to cover Bingo squares

How to Play: Prepare Bingo boards with the words students are working on. Vary the position of the words on the different boards. As you call out the words, the students check their boards and repeat each word by saying, "I have ____" before they cover the word with a chip.

This should be a fast-moving game. For a variation, a student can be the "caller."

Extension Activity

For spelling reinforcement, or to combine spelling practice with this activity, dictate the words to your students and have them set up their own boards by writing the words in random spots. For those students who have difficulty with handwriting, you can provide the words printed on squares of paper so the students can find the words and paste them on the board.

You can laminate all the boards and have your students trade boards the next time you play.

Word Slider

Objective: Students will increase the speed with which they read instructed words.

Materials: Poster board
Markers
Scissors

What to Do: Create a word slider that relates to the theme of the words students are studying. For example, if students are reading about ocean life, you could make your word slider in the shape of a crab. This is a great way to review words from the text prior to reading.

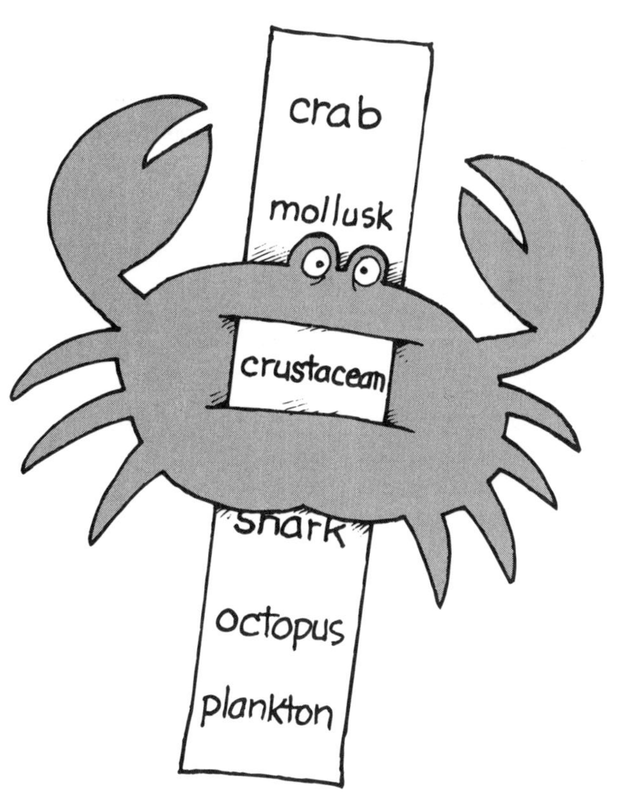

The word slider should have a window large enough to reveal one word at a time. Each student can help construct her own word slider, then practice using it by timing herself to see how fast she can read through her words.

You can also have each student keep track of how many times she practices the words by placing a sticker or a tally mark on the word slider every time she reads the words aloud to an adult; or you could have the adult initial the word slider for each reading of the words.

Sight Words

Sight Words are an essential part of every reading program. **Sight words** are words that do not follow the normal patterns or rules of decoding. Sight words are also high-frequency words that appear often in text. The activities on pages 101-108 offer ways to help your students learn and remember these often troublesome words.

There are many resources for both sight words and high-frequency words. If you don't already have such lists handy, consult www.google.com or other search engines via the Internet.

Forget-Me-Nots

Objective: Students will increase the speed with which they read sight words or high-frequency words.

Materials: Lists of sight words or high-frequency words grouped in sets of ten words

One visual reinforcer per student to keep track of progress (see pages 102-104 for examples)

What to Do: For each student, keep a list of sight words or high-frequency words posted on individual sheets in sets of ten words per sheet. After reviewing and practicing the words on a list, a student asks to be challenged when he feels ready to read his list.

This is a good way to monitor individual progress in acquiring sight words or high-frequency words. This strategy also helps motivate students to study and practice these words on their own. Use the visual reinforcers to keep track of progress. For example, have the student color a jewel in a crown (see page 102) when a set of words is mastered, or add a flower to a garden (see page 103), or add a marble to a jar (see page 104).

A student cannot be challenged on a new list the same day he receives it. Instead, he selects a previously mastered list to read.

Extension Activity

It is critical that each list of words doesn't "disappear" once a student has mastered the set. Have the student keep the lists of sight words in a notebook, in an index card file box, or on a book ring—whichever works best.

Color one jewel in the crown for each set of words you learn to read.

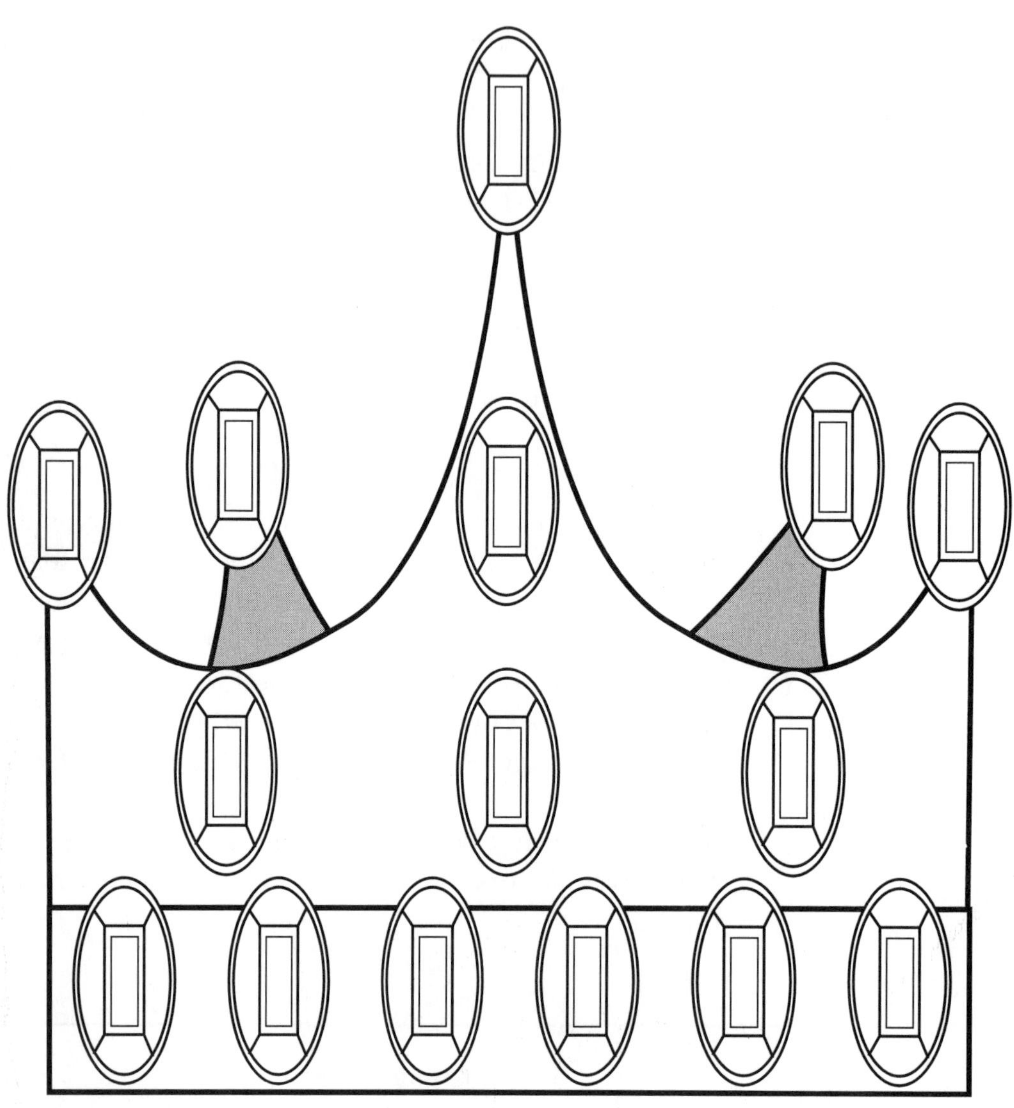

Draw a flower in the garden for each set of words you learn to read.

Add a marble to the jar for each set of words you learn to read.

Rule Breakers

Objective: Students will identify words that do not follow phonetic patterns or generalizations.

Materials: One copy of Jail for Rule Breakers (page 106)
Plain index cards, cut in half to make card strips

What to Do: Make a copy of Jail for Rule Breakers. Cut along the dotted lines to enable slipping word cards behind the "bars." You might want to laminate the "jail" before posting it on a bulletin board in your classroom. Print each sight word you wish to target on a card strip.

Explain to your students that the Jail for Rule Breakers is for words that don't follow the rules, such as *have*. Slip a few of the word strips behind the "bars" of the jail. Encourage your students to visit these important "prisoners" frequently to maintain mastery of these tricky words. Students can take a card out, read it, and then replace it back behind the bars.

Cut out the Jail for Rule Breakers below.
Use it for the activity on page 105.

Jail for Rule Breakers

Cut out all the white rectangles.

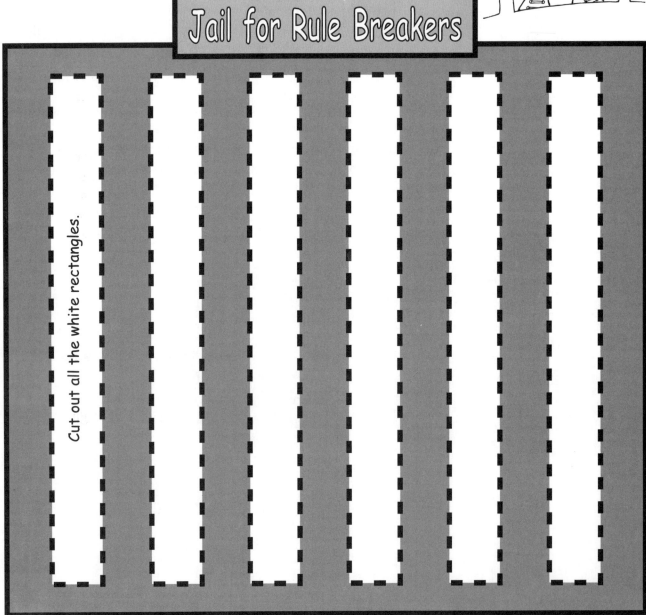

Fluency

It may be worthwhile, especially for the older students, to have a discussion about fluency and why it is important to reread stories to improve fluency. This discussion with both help to build students' metacognitive skills and improve their understanding of themselves as readers. Simply put, **metacognition** means that a student is thinking about how he learns. For instance, a student may realize that rereading words and sentences several times is the best way for him to improve his reading rate.

Rereadings

Rereading text is probably one of the best ways to improve reading fluency, but it can also be the most boring. Several ways to vary the rereadings to boost students' interest are listed below.

- ✓ Choral reading—have your students reread the story together. Explain to them that choral reading is like singing a song together, so everyone should be reading at the same pace. (This pace will increase the more they "sing" the story.) If you want to jazz up the story, the students could actually sing the story to a familiar tune, such as "Happy Birthday" or "Twinkle, Twinkle, Little Star."

- ✓ Have the students reread the story using different voices (with an accent, in a whisper, growling, etc.).

- ✓ Rewrite or manipulate the text into a play and have the kids read and act out the story.

- ✓ Substitute familiar names and places for the ones in the original story.

"Read-Aloud" Cards

Objective: After several rereadings, students will read more quickly with appropriate expression.

Materials: Index cards

What to Do: Make a set of cards with directions the students must follow as they read a passage or story aloud. Examples of such directions are printed below.

Read the story while standing on a chair.	Read the story to the school nurse.
Read the story in a whisper.	Read the story in the hallway.
Read the story into a microphone.	Read the story with an accent.
Read the story while standing on one foot.	Read the story while lying on your back.
Read the story in a monster's voice.	Read the story in a voice like your favorite character.

Fluency Phrases

Objective: Students will read more quickly with appropriate expression.

Materials: Four slips of paper per student

What to Do: Choose phrases from the passage or story that students will read and write or type them on slips of paper. Have your students sit in a circle and give each student four phrase slips. The first student reads the top phrase from his pile and then discards that slip to the bottom of the next person's pile of phrase slips. The next person reads the top phrase from her pile, discarding the phrase as soon as she has finished reading it. Keep the "circle reading" going until all the phrases have been read several times and the students' fluency has improved.

In the beginning, you will notice that the reading pace is slow and choppy, but as the phrases are passed and read, readers' fluency will improve noticeably. As they continue to read and pass their slips, their reading should become smoother and faster because the students will be rereading the phrases a number of times.

Extension Activity

After the students have practiced the phrases in the activity above, arrange your students in groups of three to five. Collect the phrases and divide them among the students. Each student takes a turn reading the top phrase on his pile. After he reads his phrase, he drops the phrase into a pile or box in the center of the circle. Use a stopwatch to time how long it takes the group to read all the phrases. As a variation, use a minute timer to see how many phrases the group can read before the minute is up. The goal is to increase the number of phrases they can read fluently (with good expression at an appropriate rate) in a minute.

Punctuation Signs

Objective: Students will heed punctuation to improve their expression as they read aloud.

Materials: Post-it notes
Yellow and red markers

What to Do: Make an analogy about punctuation that will be meaningful to your students. For example, tell them punctuation marks in text are like road signs for drivers—the periods are like *stop* signs, commas are like *yield* signs, etc. Before the students read aloud, have them highlight each period with a red marker and each comma with a yellow marker. When the students read, they should pay attention to the "signs." You can issue Post-it notes as "speeding tickets" and hand them out whenever a student races through the reading and ignores the punctuation.

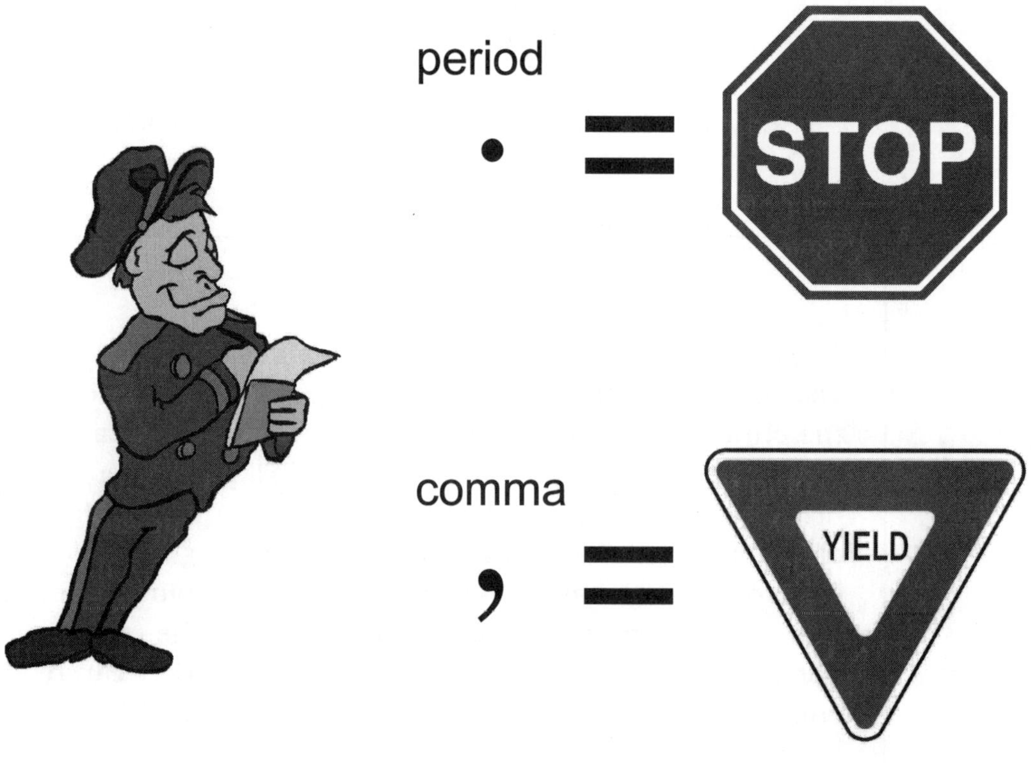

Rats! (for Phrases)

Objective: Students will increase the speed with which they read instructed phrases.

Materials: Small bucket, bowl, or bag

For each player, five to six small slips of paper with phrases printed on them (e.g., 50-60 slips for ten students)

Five to ten slips of paper with the word *Rats!* printed on them (or copy the template below)

What to Do: Fold all the slips of paper and place them into the bucket, bowl, or bag. Each student takes a turn pulling out the slips of paper and reading the phrases. If she draws a *Rats!*, she must read all the slips she has acquired, then put them back into the bucket, bowl, or bag. The first player to collect five phrase slips wins.

Señor or Señorita Speedy

Objective: Students will read a passage as fast as they can.

Materials: Stories or text that the students are reading for class

What to Do: After the students have read a story or article, challenge them to be "Señor Speedy" or "Señorita Speedy" and read the story as fast as possible. The point of this activity is for the student to read as fast as possible, not worrying about punctuation.

This is a fun way to end a reading period!

Practice Points

Objective: Students will improve their reading fluency (fast, expressive reading).

Materials: A photo-copy of a story or article that the students are reading

One copy of Practice Points (page 114) per student

What to Do: Each day the student takes his reading from class home and practices reading to himself and to others. Each time he reads to himself, he puts a tally mark in the box marked *I have practiced reading to myself this many times.*

Each time the student reads to someone, that person initials the box marked *I have practiced reading to someone this many times.*

You can count the marks and initials as points towards a certain goal. Keep a record of the points posted in your classroom. If you have a particularly competitive group, you may want to have your students work collectively toward a class goal, or you can set a goal for the class. For example, you could challenge your students to earn 50 practice points by the end of the week.

Practice Points

Name ______________________________

Every time you read to yourself, make a tally mark in the box below.

I have practiced reading to myself this many times.

Every time you read to someone, have that person write his or her initials in the box below.

I have practiced reading to someone this many times.

Read Racer

Objective: Students will improve their reading fluency (fast, expressive reading).

Materials: Racecar cutouts (see below)
Read Racer Speedway (page 116)
One file folder per student
Stories or reading material
Timer

What to Do: Each student has her own racetrack and car. We suggest putting the racetrack into a file folder so that the student can keep this folder handy in school or at home.

The student practices reading a passage, story, or article silently. When she is ready to "get into the driver's seat," she pairs up with a partner and reads.

Her partner times her reading and records the time on the "starting line." The first reading establishes the starting time. If her time improves the next time she reads, she moves to "Lap 2." Each time her speed improves, the time is recorded on the track and she advances a lap. She should continue rereading the same story until she makes it around the track by improving her time each turn.

The partners should take turns reading. This activity should not be completed in one sitting, but rather, the student can hop "back into the driver's seat" after practicing.

time:
LAP 2
LAP 1
time:
Read Racer
Speedway
LAP 3
time:
LAP 4
time:
Start
Finish

News Reporter

Objective: Students will improve their reading fluency when reading "real world" reading materials, such as newspapers, school menus, weather reports, etc.

Materials: Local newspaper or magazine
Everyday reading materials

What to Do: Students take turns being the "news reporter" for the week. The student's job has these responsibilities:

- ✓ Read the weather report for the day.
- ✓ Read the lunch menu.
- ✓ Read the news headline and captions.

If there is a follow-up article each day, encourage the student to stick with that topic. Continuous exposure to the same names and vocabulary will enhance automaticity and fluency.

By reading the weather and menu each day, the student will become increasingly familiar with specific vocabulary. For example, a student who can only read short-vowel words will expand his reading vocabulary to such words as *cloudy*, *pleasant*, and *drizzle*. Likewise, the words from the school menu are often repeated throughout the year, such as *hamburger*, *vegetable*, and *dessert*. Students are more likely to master these words with repeated, frequent exposure.

Class Expert

Objective: Students will improve their reading fluency when reading expository text.

Materials: Expository text, preferably from students' textbooks

What to Do: Have your students choose a topic of interest. Each student will research information. (Help students find appropriate information or provide such information for them.) Then each student will read the information and write a short summary of the information.

Each student will then practice reading her summary several times (see Practice Points on page 113). Select a day when the "expert" will present the information to the group. Each student will read her summary fluently.

This is a wonderful activity to improve fluency while teaching public speaking skills. You can give the student feedback using the chart below. Circle the appropriate numbers.

Expert: ______________________________

Topic: ______________________________

Date: ______________

1 = needs work   2 = well done   3 = EXCELLENT!

Reading Fluency	1	2	3
Volume	1	2	3
Eye Contact	1	2	3

"Ol' Favorites"

Objective: Students will improve their reading fluency.

Materials: One three-ring binder per student

What to Do: For each student, keep a copy of every story, article, word list, etc., read throughout the year in a three-ring binder. Encourage your students to reread their favorites from over the year. Not only is this a great resource for rereadings, but it will also motivate the students as they watch their binders "grow."

The binder is also a great resource to give to anyone who will be working with a student. The binder can be used for reading practice during school breaks and summer vacation.

4 Reading Comprehension

Just as automaticity and fluency are the goals for decoding instruction, reading for meaning is the purpose of all reading instruction. Many students who have acquired decoding skills, however, still struggle to understand what they read. These students need strategies to help them comprehend written material.

Reading for meaning is an active process that begins as soon as a student picks up a book or turns a page. We need to help our students become active readers before, during, and after they read. Our help often begins with a conversation that enables students to tap into their background knowledge about a subject. Vocabulary instruction that occurs simultaneously with reading is an effective way to increase a students' understanding of text. Strategies such as visualizing, questioning, rereading, and summarizing all help to make text meaningful to students as they interact with reading materials.

The following guidelines are key to the activities in this chapter.

Capitalize on students' interests.

- ✓ Take interest inventories at the beginning of the year (see sample inventory, page 122).
- ✓ Get to know your students and what they are interested in learning.
- ✓ Find out what your students like to read for pleasure, such as specific magazines, newspaper sections, or novels.
- ✓ Develop thematic units that extend beyond students' textbooks. Link the decoding material to higher level, uncontrolled material.

Use lots of repetition.

- ✓ You need to model for your students and give them guided practice before they will be able to use good comprehension strategies on their own.
- ✓ Practice each strategy in a variety of ways until the student can apply the strategy independently without being prompted. Keep in mind, this is a long-term goal for many students who have comprehension difficulties.
- ✓ Use a variety of materials for strategy practice. For example, use both fiction and nonfiction materials.

Focus on comprehension, not assessment.

- ✓ Use the strategies to develop students' understanding of material. Do not use the strategies as a substitute for formal or informal assessment of students' reading comprehension.
- ✓ Keep your students' needs in mind. You may have to begin at a picture or sentence-by-sentence level, then build up to paragraphs, then to whole passages or stories.
- ✓ Help students find those comprehension strategies that work best for them. For example, some students are more visual than others, so drawing pictures is a great strategy for them as they read.

Reading Interest Inventory

Name ______________________________ Date ___________________

For each question, write what you think. There are no right or wrong answers.

I read approximately _________ times a week.

I spend approximately _________ minutes reading each week.

My favorite place to read is ____

I like to read these kinds of things: (Circle each one you like to read.)

books magazines books on tape

newspapers book series Internet other ____________

I like to read books about ____

My favorite book so far is ____

The hardest thing about reading is ___________________________________

____

When I get to a word I don't know, I __________________________________

____

When I don't understand something I am reading, I ______________________

____

This year I would like to read more about ______________________________

____

Pre-Reading Strategies

Motivating your students to read can be challenging. Pre-reading activities are essential to spark interest in a book. Many students bring a variety of personal experiences and a wealth of background knowledge into the classroom. It is our role as teachers to help students access this information and make connections with the reading.

We need to help students with limited organization or background knowledge to make connections in some way. For example, suppose the class is going to read about sharks. Some students will have visited aquariums or even have gone deep sea fishing; other students may not have even seen an ocean. We must include all of the students by relating some aspect of their personal experiences or opinions to the topic. Here are some options:

Teacher: How many of you have seen a shark? (Many students raise their hands and talk about visits to aquariums, etc.)

Teacher: (Shows a picture of a great white shark to draw in all of the students) Has anyone ever seen a picture of a great white shark?

Teacher: Some people study sharks by going underwater in a steel cage. Would you ever want to do that? (Many students will be able to imagine or visualize themselves in this situation and share their feelings about it.)

Always use visuals to introduce a new topic. For example, if the class will read about bald eagles, have plenty of books about birds in your classroom for students to refer to. Posters, photos, the Internet, and magazines are also wonderful ways to stimulate students' interest and get them ready to read.

The activities in this part of Chapter 4 will inspire your students to know more about what they will read. Many of the activities will help students inquire about a topic. Giving them a structure to organize their thoughts and questions before reading helps students become active learners. They will want to find out the answers to their questions. Similarly, getting to know more about a specific author can provide insight into why the author wrote about a topic. Also included in this chapter are activities that instruct and reinforce vocabulary to further develop students' understanding of the text. These activities will immerse your students in the excitement of reading!

Book Hook

Objective: Teachers will entice their students by introducing "hooks" that are related to the topic of the text.

Materials: The materials you choose will depend on the text. For example, if you are introducing a book about Sir Edmund Hillary, you may want to bring a bag of camping/climbing equipment or magazine pictures of the Himalayas or climbing expeditions.

What to Do: You can present "book hooks" in a variety of ways.

✓ You can leave them out on a table in your classroom, first thing in the morning as your students enter the room.

✓ Begin a problem-solving discussion about the objects, such as, "Imagine you are going on a trip to the Himalayas. You can only pack five things for your trip. What will you take? Will you bring a bathing suit?"

✓ Some of the objects may be exotic foods. For example, if the text will be about the rainforest, you could bring in a tropical fruit. If you will be reading about climbing the Himalayas, bring in some unfamiliar or unusual tools, such as crampons or carabiners. See if your students can guess what the foods or objects are. Encourage them to share any relevant experiences or do some research to discover what the things are and how they are used.

✓ Maps are a great way to integrate geography skills with text your students will read.

✓ Bring in an expert to talk about personal experiences or expertise that relates to what your students will read.

K-W-L Chart

Objective: Students will access their background knowledge of a topic, brainstorm questions they have about the topic, and then review all that they learned about the topic.

Materials: Chart (see below)

What to Do: This strategy comes from D. M. Ogle, 1986. On an overhead or the board, make a chart like the one below. In the first column, list all the information students already KNOW about the subject. In the second column, list students' questions about what they WANT to know. After students read the text, list what the students LEARNED from reading the text.

Encourage students who can write independently to make their own charts and log their information. Consider having students share their thoughts by working in small groups. The group can do a K-W-L chart as a team project, pooling their resources.

Topic:

Know	Want to Know	Learned

Pre-reading Discussions

Objective: Students will develop background knowledge on a specific topic prior to reading.

Materials: Books, maps, charts, crafts, photographs, props, illustrations, food, posters, etc.

What to Do: Before your students read something, present information and have discussions to help your students anticipate the reading and understand the topic. For example, if your students will read *Sadako and the Thousand Paper Cranes* by Eleanor Coerr, present the following information for your students to browse through and talk about:

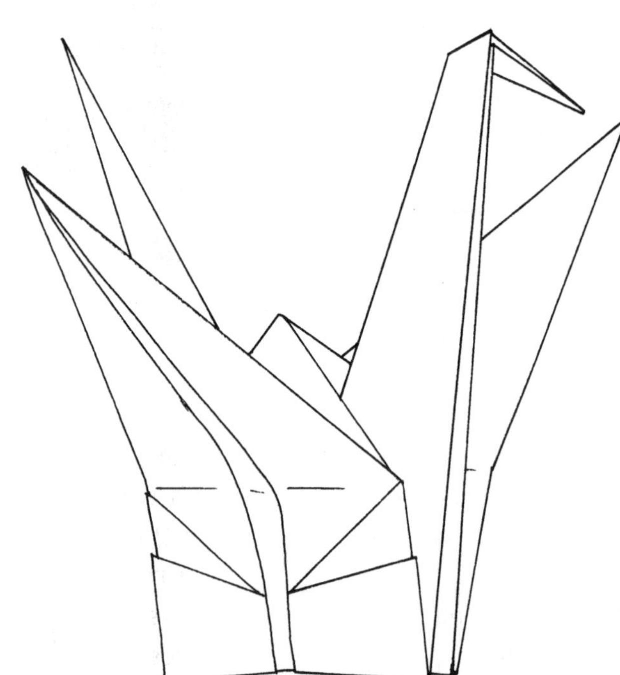

World War II

World War II, Eyewitness Books by Simon Adams

America Goes to War by John Devaney

Japan

Japan, Children of the World Series

My Hiroshima by Junko Morimoto

Hiroshima, No Pika by Toshi Maruki

Shin's Tricycle by Tatsuharu Kodama

Origami

Origami Animals by Hector Rojas

Papercrafts Around the World by Phyllis and Noel Fiarotta

Reading Expedition

Objective: Students will become motivated to read stories that are set all over the world. They will work toward a goal of hitting all the continents, a certain number of countries, or countries of their ancestors, etc.

Materials: Large world map posted in the classroom or in the hall

Push pins or place markers (clip art of a boat, airplane, and bus)

Post-it notes to label the titles they have read

What to Do: Before you begin a new book or article with your students, discuss the setting of the article. Using the world map, place a marker (i.e., push pin, clip art) in the location of the story. Lead a discussion comparing and contrasting that part of the world with your own area.

Extension Activity

Spend some time getting to know each country. Have your students do some research. One student could research the climate, another could learn about the foods, etc. Have the students present this information for their peers. Encourage each presenter to use visual aides (pictures, maps, objects, posters, etc.) to boost other students' interest in each presentation.

I Wonder Book (for nonfiction)

Objective: Students will become active readers by asking questions about topics they want to read about.

Materials: One composition book per student

What to Do: This is a journal writing activity that supports inquiry. Ask your students to list all the questions they have about a specific topic. This list can be ongoing—before, during, and after reading—or it can be a random list with students brainstorming questions about a certain topic every morning.

Extension Activity

Have the students go back into their I Wonder Books and answer their questions after they have read something on their topics.

Brainstorming Web

Objective: Students will access and organize their background information about a specific topic onto a graphic organizer.

Materials: See below and pages 130-131 for examples of webs. Inspiration software is a wonderful tool to use for this activity—*Inspiration Version 6.0* (1988-2000), Inspiration Software.

What to Do: Students use a graphic organizer to record information they know about a certain topic. Students can use this information to write a prediction paragraph about a character in the story or about an event that may take place.

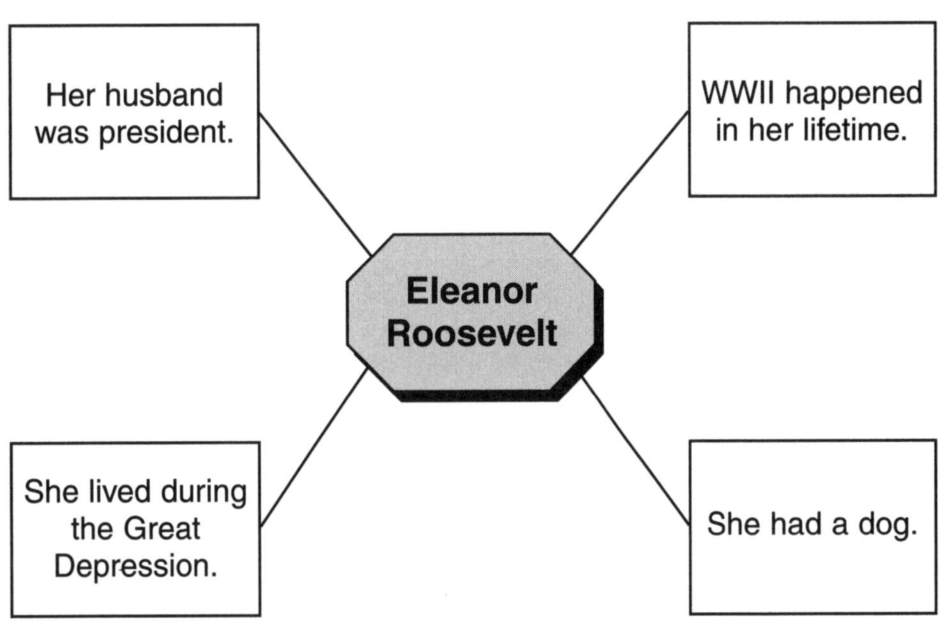

Extension Activity

Give your students a focus question to guide their reading based on their brainstorming webs. For example, using the web above, the focus question could be *What was Eleanor Roosevelt's role during WWII?*

Use this web to organize information about what you read.

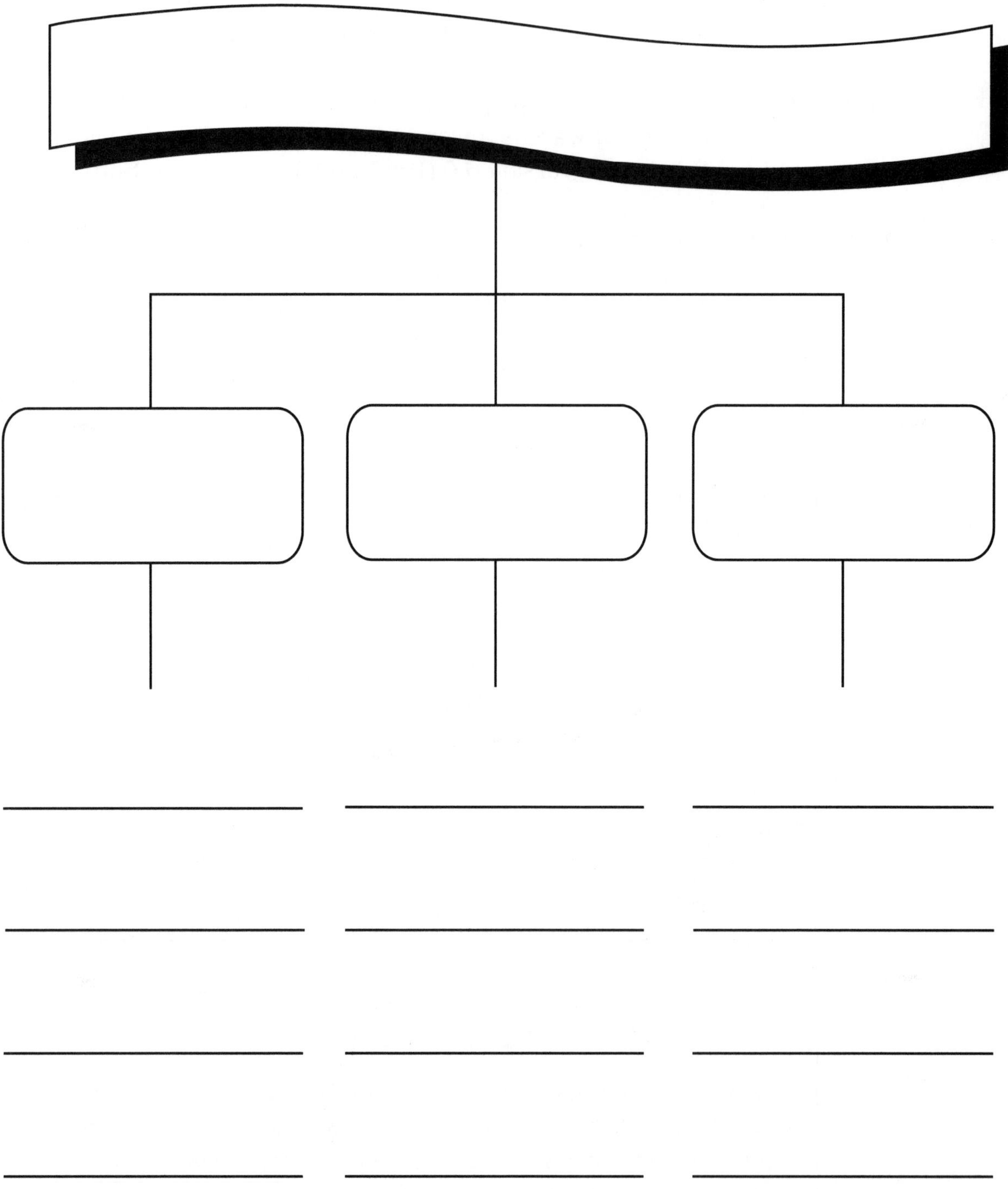

Use this web to organize information about what you read.

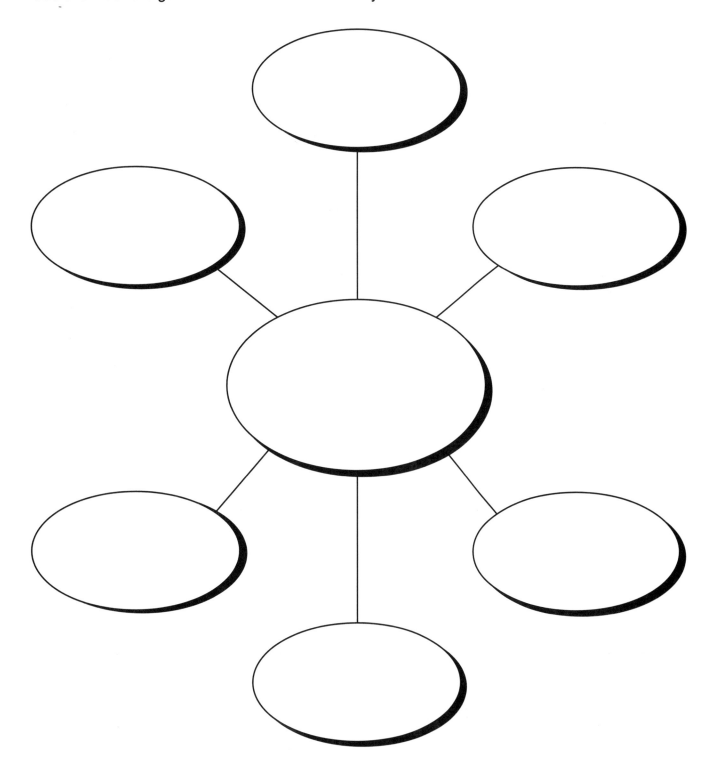

Applauding an Author

Objective: Students will learn about a particular author before they read a book written by that author.

Materials: Information about an author
One copy of Applauding an Author (page 133) per student

What to Do: Have your students study a particular author. They can find information in the library or via the Internet. Each student is to fill in five facts in the illustration (see example below). Then students can use these facts to write brief summaries about their author(s) and present this information to the class. This project can be done as a class or each student can do independent research to "applaud" an author.

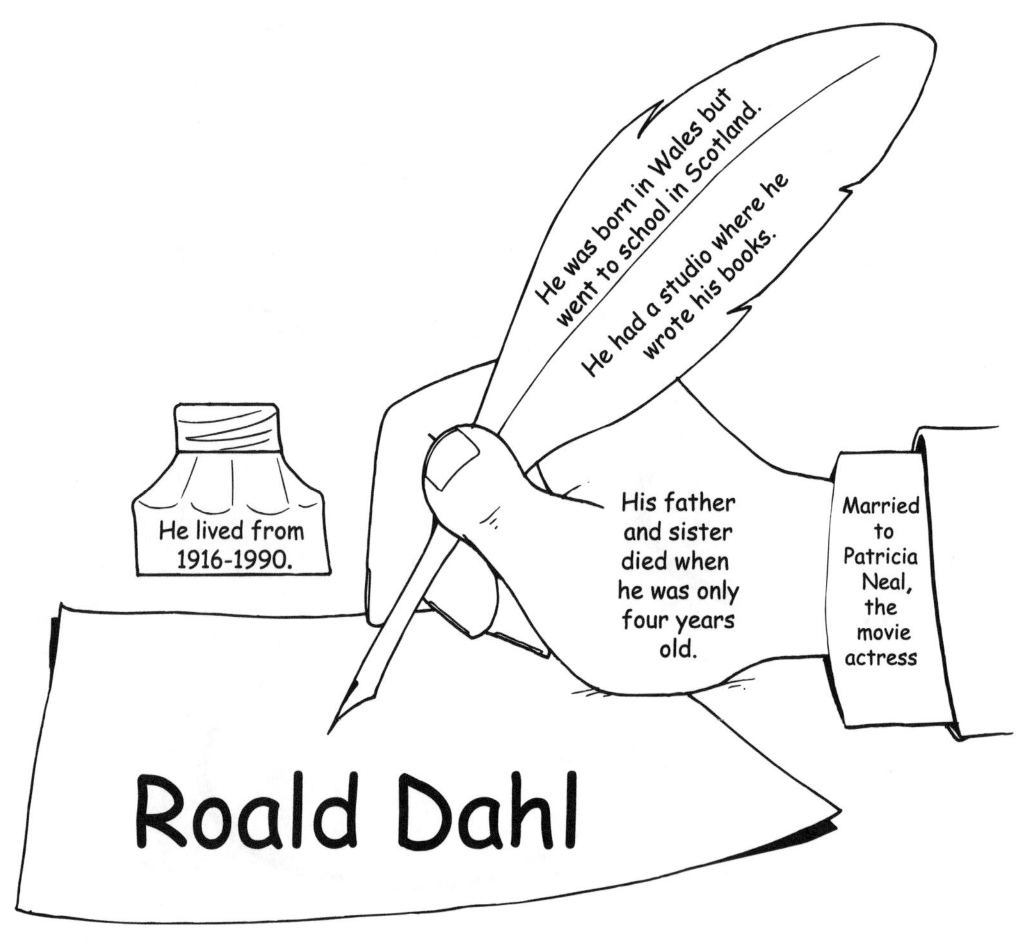

Applauding an Author

Write five facts about an author in this outline. Then write a brief summary about the author.

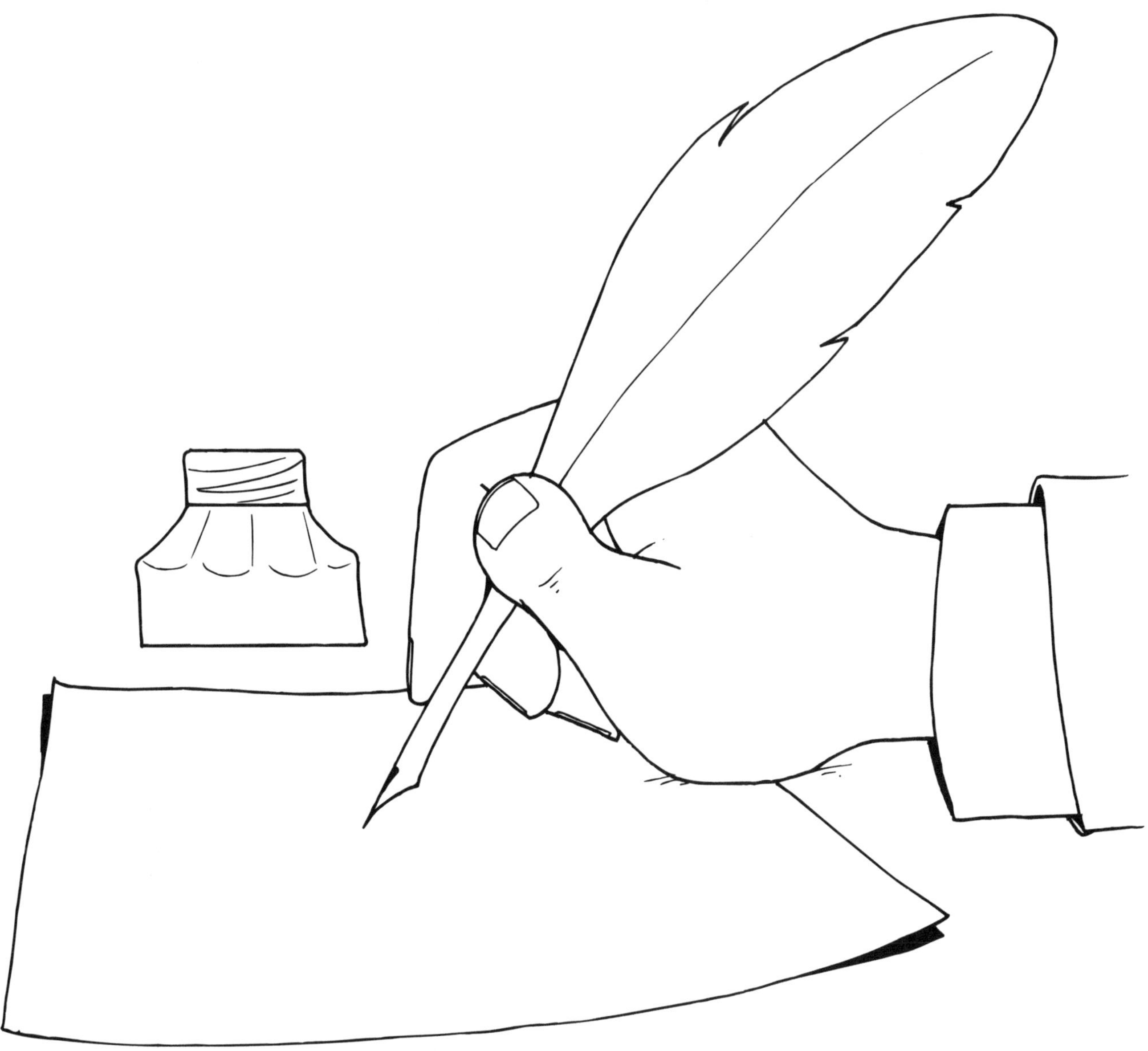

Vocabulary Games

Games are an engaging way to help students identify and define unfamiliar vocabulary that they will encounter in their reading. Once you have presented the vocabulary, review will be necessary to enhance students' comprehension and to ensure their ability to generalize the vocabulary in their daily work.

Vocabulary Bingo

Objective: Students will identify and define unfamiliar vocabulary they encounter in reading.

Materials: One copy of Vocabulary Bingo (page 136) per student
Chips or pennies
Index cards with definitions printed on one side

What to Do: Write the definitions of 24 target words on separate index cards. Write the same words on each Bingo board, varying the order of the words. Give each student a Bingo board and a handful of chips. Read a definition. Then each student looks to see if she has the vocabulary word anywhere on her board. If she does, she covers the word with a chip.

The first student to get five in a row (vertical, horizontal, or diagonal) shouts, "Bingo!" You can continue playing the game for "Blackout," which means the entire Bingo board must be covered to end the game.

Vocabulary Bingo				
volcano	crust	tides	saline	plate
Pangea	erupt	core	fault	trench
crest	fold	**FREE**	mantle	island
valley	tremor	igneous	cone	strata
sediment	magma	mineral	gem	lava

Extension Activity

Have the students create the definition cards as an assignment before they play the game.

Vocabulary Bingo

		FREE		

Vocabulary Wheel

Objective: Students will identify and define unfamiliar vocabulary they encounter in reading.

Materials: Poster board
Brad fastener
Spinner

What to Do: Make a Vocabulary Wheel from poster board (see example below).

Ask your students to take turns spinning the Vocabulary Wheel. When the spinner stops, the student is to say the correct response. For example, if the spinner lands on *antonym* for the vocabulary word *fragile*, the student should respond with *strong*, *sturdy*, or a similar word. This activity can be done in a small group or students can pair up.

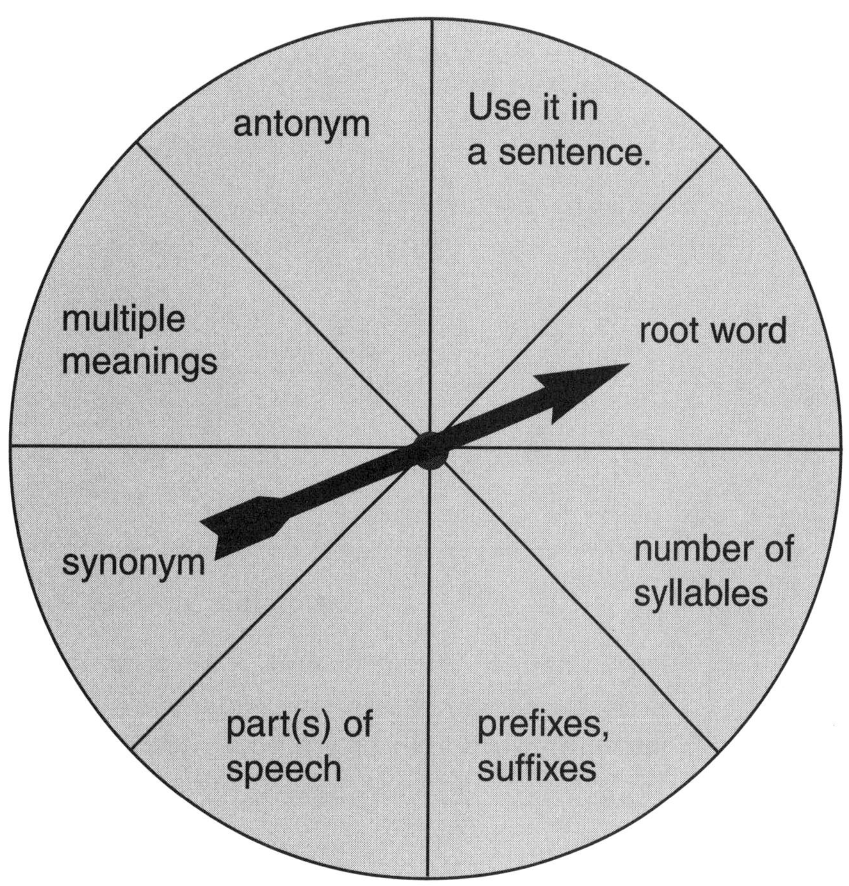

Vocabulary Charades

Objective: Students will identify and define unfamiliar vocabulary they encounter in reading.

Materials: Vocabulary word list from reading material

What to Do: Give each student a turn acting out one of his vocabulary words. A student acts out his word while the other students in the class try to guess what vocabulary word he is acting out. In the example below, the student is pantomiming the word *enthusiasm.*

Extension Activity

For a change, tape a vocabulary word on the back of a student and have the other students explain the word while he determines the vocabulary word being described.

Vocabulary Categorizing Activities

Objective: Students will identify and define unfamiliar vocabulary they encounter in reading.

Materials: Index cards with target words written on them

What to Do: Vocabulary categorizing activities can take many different forms. You can ask the students to categorize their vocabulary words by function, part of speech, beginning sound, number of syllables, etc. For example, using the words from the Bingo board on page 135, you could make several categories.

One-Syllable Words

crust
tides
plate
core
fault
trench
crest
fold
cone
gem

Two-Syllable Words

saline
erupt
mantle
island
valley
tremor
strata
magma
lava

Three-Syllable Words

volcano
Pangea
igneous
sediment
mineral

Classroom Vocabulary Balderdash

Objective: Students will identify and define unfamiliar vocabulary they encounter in reading.

Materials: Index cards
Vocabulary list

What to Do: Use this activity when your students are first learning the definitions of new words. Divide the students into two teams. Team One selects a vocabulary word and each team member writes a made-up definition, including the real one. Then Team One tells Team Two the word and reads each definition. Team Two needs to guess which definition is the real one. If Team Two guesses the real definition, it earns a point. If not, Team One earns the point. Below is an example for the word *terrain*; the correct definition is card number three.

Definition 1

The small drops of water before a torrential rainstorm

Definition 2

The eastern part of Pakistan

Definition 3

The surface features of a tract of land

Definition 4

A carriage-like vehicle used to transport goods from one place to another

During-Reading Activities

Engaging your students in activities while they are reading is probably one of the most important exercises you can do to develop your students' comprehension. Predicting, visualizing, questioning, and summarizing through role play and discussion are effective strategies for reading for meaning. Predicting activities, much like the pre-reading activities previously discussed, help to motivate readers and provide anticipatory sets for their reading. This difficult skill needs to be taught explicitly to students.

On the following pages, you will find activities to help students understand the concept of visualizing and to begin to develop their ability to form mental pictures that correspond with their reading. However, not all students are able to visualize, so some will need to learn other comprehension strategies that will work for them.

Questioning and summarizing activities are also presented in this chapter. These activities can address all levels of comprehension: literal, interpretive, creative, and critical. You will need to keep in mind your students' levels of comprehension skills so you can modify activities accordingly. For example, many students may need guided questioning in order to answer higher-level comprehension questions.

> Remember that helping your students learn to read for meaning and to interact with text is the purpose of all reading instruction.

Time Capsule Predicting

Objective: Students will use information from a story to draw logical conclusions about the events in the story.

Materials: Cardboard canister
Construction paper
Markers
Paper

What to Do: This activity can be done as a whole group, with a partner, or as an individual project. Students are to design a time capsule into which everyone's story predictions will be placed until the students have read the end of the story. Revisit the ideas after the reading to see if the predictions were accurate.

Visualizing with Wordless Picture Books

Objective: Students will understand the concept of visualizing after interacting with wordless picture books.

Materials: Post-it notes

Wordless picture books such as the examples listed below:

Banyai, I. *Zoom.* New York: Viking, 1995.
Banyai, I. *Re-Zoom.* New York: Viking, 1995.
Briggs, R. *The Snowman.* New York: Viking, 1978.
Day, A. *Good Dog Carl.* New York: Simon & Schuster, 1997.
dePaola, T. *Knight and the Dragon.* New York: G.P. Putnam's Sons, 1980.
Schories, P. *Mouse Around.* Canada: Harper-Collins, 1991.
Turkle, B. *Deep in the Forest.* New York: Dutton, 1976.
Wiesner, D. *Free Fall.* New York: Lothrop, Lee & Shepard Books, 1988.

What to Do: This is a great, concrete way to demonstrate and teach visualizing. As you teach your students to use the pictures of a story to create the text, you are actually asking them to do the opposite of visualizing. Students are asked to either tell or write a story based on the pictures in the books listed above. You can have your students do this activity independently or in pairs. Each student can use Post-it notes right in the book to write the text of the story. Then the students can share their text that explains the story the illustrations tell.

Visualizing

Objective: Students will form mental pictures that correspond with their reading.

Materials: Paper
Pencil, pen, colored pencil, or marker for each student

What to Do: Have your students close their eyes and listen to a piece of descriptive text. Tell them to try to "make a movie in their heads" and then ask the students to describe orally what they visualized. Let artistic students draw what they visualized, and then have the students discuss and compare their images. You can use felt boards as a medium for students who are less artistic. Simple shapes can represent the images in the text. The example below is for the poem *Band-Aid Andy*.

Band-Aid Andy

Andy was so excited to go outside,

He hopped on his bike and went for a ride.

He picked up speed as he sped down a hill,

And at the bottom, he took a great spill.

Now he wears Band-Aids from head to toe.

Next time, perhaps, he'll take it slow!

Questioning Techniques

Teaching students to ask questions while they are reading will help them become more active, thoughtful readers. For many students who have comprehension difficulties, this skill needs to be taught explicitly.

At first, students may benefit from teacher modeling of questioning. For example, in the middle of a paragraph, you might stop and ask aloud, "Now what's happening to the main character? Where is she?"

The worksheets and activities in this section provide opportunities for students to practice answering questions of their reading independently. Asking questions helps students identify the main idea of what they are reading. Gathering this information will then help them summarize what they have read and enable them to engage in higher-level comprehension activities, such as relating to characters, making inferences, and providing an opinion. Role-playing activities provide opportunities for students to ask questions in a more creative way.

The activities on the following pages provide ways to include questioning techniques as part of your comprehension instruction.

Five W's Cube

Objective: Students will ask questions to determine the important details of the text while reading.

Materials: Cardboard box, covered die, or paper cube with the six sides labeled *who, what, when, where, why*, and *how*

What to Do: Have students toss the cube and take turns asking each other questions about the story. Below are some example questions for the story *Hoot* by Carl Hiaasen:

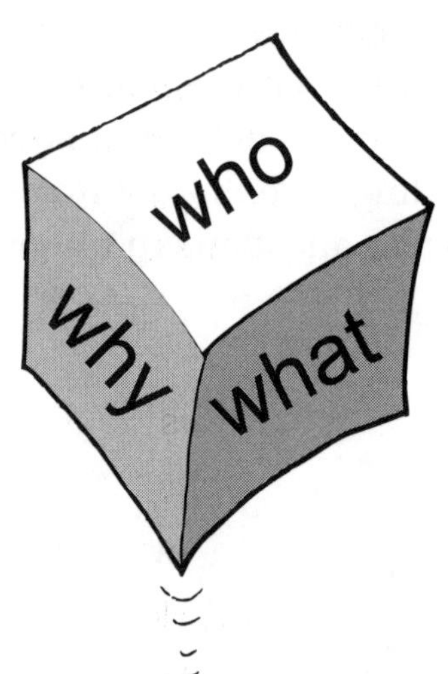

WHO was the boy running along the sidewalk, with no backpack and no shoes?

WHAT happened to the stakes at the construction site?

WHERE did the story take place?

WHEN did Roy meet Mullet Fingers?

WHY were Roy, Mullet Fingers, and Beatrice trying to stop the construction?

HOW did you feel when the owls were saved?

For students who have difficulty formulating questions, model and practice questioning by having your students toss the cube and ask each other questions about their weekends, their families, their favorite things, etc.

Get the Facts, Jack

Objective: Students will determine the main gist of their reading by asking the five *wh* and *how* questions.

Materials: One Get the Facts, Jack (page 148) per student
Butcher block paper
Markers

What to Do: Using butcher block paper, create a chart of six boxes, each with a question word (*Who, What, When, Where, Why, How*) or use the sample worksheet on page 148. As the students read an article or paragraph, they answer questions to fill in their fact chart, such as *Who is the article about?, Where does it take place?,* and *When is it happening?* It is helpful if students use a highlighter or underline as they are reading to highlight the *wh* information in their reading. The passage below is an example of such highlighting.

Johnny Appleseed was born in Massachusetts in 1774. His real name was John Chapman. Johnny liked to wander away from home and take long walks into the woods, where he studied the habits of the birds and the animals. When he was about twenty five, he **walked** to the Ohio River valley and began his **life's work**. He became a preacher and **he planted apple trees all through the frontier**. **His apple trees fed all the people who were going west**. He continued planting apple trees for almost **fifty years until he was seventy-five years old**. He was a familiar figure to the pioneers and the Indians.

Who Johnny Appleseed	**What** planted apple trees
Where all through the frontier	**When** from the age of 25-75
Why He wanted to feed the people headed out West.	**How** walked

Get the Facts, Jack

WHO is the story mainly about?
WHAT is the most important thing that is happening?
WHERE are the events taking place?
WHEN are the events of the story taking place?
WHY is this important in the story?
HOW are the events of the story taking place?

Who	**What**
Where	**When**
Why	**How**

Teacher Time

Objective: Students will become familiar with asking questions and leading discussions.

Materials: Reading material (expository or narrative text)

Nine index cards labeled *predicting*, *clarifying*, or *summarizing* (three of each type)

Hat

What to Do: During a discussion, model good questioning techniques for your students. Your questions should focus on different comprehension skills, such as summarizing, predicting, and clarifying. Identify the specific skill clearly for each question. Then the students take turns pulling a question card out of a hat and become the teacher by asking their questions and leading the discussion. Example questions below illustrate this activity.

Topic: Mount Everest

Predicting questions

Do you think they will find clues that the Yeti really exists?

How do you think Norgay and Hillary's expedition ended?

Clarifying questions

Did Sir Edmund Hillary climb Everest before or after he climbed another mountain?

Was Tenzing Norgay from Nepal or Tibet?

Summarizing questions

How are expeditions to Everest today different from Norgay and Hillary's climb in 1953?

What impact did Norgay and Hillary's expedition have on Mount Everest?

Question Cube

Objective: Students will formulate critical comprehension questions during and after reading a paragraph, section, or passage (depending on the level of your students).

Materials: Cardboard box or paper cube with the six sides labeled *Summarize, Detail, Predict, Infer, Relate,* and *Opinion*

What to Do: Have students toss the cube and take turns asking each other corresponding questions about the text. The questions below are examples based on *Holes* by Louis Sachar.

Summarize Summarize how Stanley ended up at Camp Green Lake.

Detail Provide one detail about one of the boys in Stanley's cabin at the juvenile detention center.

Predict What do you think will happen to Zero?

Infer From all the foreshadowing about the dangers of the yellow spotted lizards, do you think someone will get bitten by one?

Relate How is this camp the same or different from a camp you have attended?

Opinion In your opinion, is it fair to send children to youth detention camps?

Character Talk Show

Objective: Students will answer questions about a story character or an "expert."

Materials: Handheld microphone

What to Do: Have one student, or several students, play the roles of the major characters in the story. The other class members can be the hosts or audience members who ask the questions, using a handheld microphone. Everyone gets the opportunity to ask questions of the characters by passing the microphone around. If you are reading expository text, a student can play the role of the "expert."

The example below relates to *Hatchet* by Gary Paulsen.

Main Idea Activities

In order to help your students accurately recognize the main idea of what they read, you first need to determine the level at which to begin your instruction: sentence by sentence, paragraph, passage, or chapter level. If a student is having difficulty identifying what a chapter is about, you may need to review the chapter one page at a time. If this approach is still difficult, have the student engage in an activity at the paragraph level.

Determining the main idea is essential for students to be able to summarize what they have read. Using expository text may make it easier for some students to determine the main facts of an article. Fiction can be more challenging because it involves characters, settings, and conflicts. Consider this difference when selecting material for main idea instruction.

Once students have determined the main idea of what they have read, they can begin to identify the supporting details. Supporting details provide more information about the topic of the story.

The activities on the following pages provide a variety of ways to help students determine the main idea of what they are reading. This skill will facilitate students' ability to summarize and retell a passage or story in their own words.

Running Log

Objective: Students will identify the main ideas in reading material.

Materials: One copy of Main Idea Log (page 154) per student

What to Do: Have your students keep a running log of the main ideas in the story. You will need to model and help your students determine main idea vs. details. This determination can be done at the paragraph, page, or chapter level, depending on the needs of your students. The example below and the Main Idea Log involve identifying main ideas of paragraphs.

Main Idea Log

Title/Chapter: Wolves

Paragraph: 1 Main Idea: The population of wolves has increased because a program has relocated wolves out West.

Paragraph: 2 Main Idea: Wolves were almost hunted to extinction.

Paragraph: 3 Main Idea: Now wolves are threatening farmers' livestock.

Main Idea Log

Title/Chapter: ______________________________

Paragraph: ______ Main Idea: ______________________________

____

Paragraph: ______ Main Idea: ______________________________

____

Paragraph: ______ Main Idea: ______________________________

____

Paragraph: ______ Main Idea: ______________________________

____

Paragraph: ______ Main Idea: ______________________________

____

Paragraph: ______ Main Idea: ______________________________

____

Paragraph: ______ Main Idea: ______________________________

____

Stickies

Objective: Students will identify the main ideas in a chapter. Depending on your students' skills, you can do this activity at a paragraph, page, or chapter level.

Materials: One pad of Post-it notes per student

What to Do: Give each student a pad of Post-it notes. As a student finishes a paragraph, page, or chapter, he can record the main idea on a Post-it and attach it right on the book page or reading material. If the chapters are not titled, the student can also use the stickies to give each chapter a title based on the main idea. The example below is based on *Maniac Magee* by Jerry Spinelli, page 54.

Title It

Objective: Students will identify the main ideas in a paragraph. (You can do this activity at a paragraph, page, or chapter level, depending on your students' skills.)

Materials: One copy of Becoming a Puppy Owner (page 157) and/or Shackleton (page 158) per student

What to Do: Give each student a copy of one of the worksheets. Tell your students that each title in the box is the main idea of one of the paragraphs on the worksheet. Read the titles with your students.

Next read one paragraph at a time on the worksheet and ask your students to choose the best title for that paragraph from the choices on the worksheet. Ask students to explain how they know that is the best title.

Once your students are able to identify the main idea of a paragraph when choices are provided, work toward increased independence for this skill. Some students might benefit from working with a partner or in a small group before tackling this task by themselves.

You can use a variety of interesting reading material for this training. Students' textbooks are a great resource. You can also cut out short articles from news magazines such as *Time for Kids* or *Scholastic News*. Ask your students to give each paragraph a title.

For reverse practice, list a few titles or main ideas and have your students write a brief paragraph that goes with one of the items on the list.

Becoming a Puppy Owner

Read each paragraph. Then choose the title from the box that tells the main idea of each paragraph. Write the letter in the blank beside the paragraph.

a. Giving Your Puppy More Space
b. Supplies for Your Dog
c. Keeping Your Puppy Safe
d. How to Get a Puppy
e. Preparing Your Home

1. ____ There are many ways in which you can get a pet. You can go to dog shows, talk to breeders, visit pet shops, go to a pound, or talk with friends. Learning all the different options will help you decide which one is best for you.

2. ____ Before you bring your new puppy home, it is important to puppy-proof your house. Puppies are a lot like babies; they're curious and they can get into a lot of trouble very fast! One of the first things you'll need to do is buy some baby gates. The gates will limit the amount of space your puppy has to run around the house.

3. ____ Introduce the puppy to more space one step at a time. Start with one small room (bathroom, laundry room) and work up to the family room.

4. ____ Next you'll need to look around the room and think, "What would a puppy chew on?" Put anything fragile or dangerous (cords, cleaning chemicals, small pieces of toys) away.

5. ____ Lastly, you'll need to get some supplies for your new puppy. You will need a leash and a collar. You may want to crate-train your puppy, or you may want to get a dog bed. When you want to buy toys for your dog, make sure they are dog toys. The most important thing you can get for your puppy is an identification tag. Remember, proper identification is not only important; it's the law!

Answers: 1d, 2e, 3a, 4c, 5b

Shackleton

Read each paragraph. Then choose the title from the box that tells the main idea of each paragraph. Write the letter in the blank beside the paragraph.

a. *The Endurance* Is Stuck

b. The Expedition

c. The Crew Abandons the Ship

d. The Crew

1. ____ On August 8, 1914, Sir Ernest Shackleton and his crew set sail from England aboard *The Endurance*. Shackleton was the leader of the Imperial Trans-Antarctic Expedition. He and his crew were sailing to Antarctica in hopes of becoming the first explorers to cross the icy continent.

2. ____ Shackleton was careful in choosing his crew. There were 28 men in all—a few scientists, two doctors, a carpenter, and a cook. There were also several animals aboard—a cat, two pigs, and 69 sled dogs. In addition, the ship was packed with two years' worth of food.

3. ____ Not long into the journey, the ship became stuck in the ice. The crew tried to release the ship by chopping the ice around it, but it was useless. They were stuck until the weather turned warmer.

4. ____ The pressure from the ice around the ship's hull became greater and greater. It was apparent that the ship was being crushed. The men had to evacuate the ship and continue their journey on foot. They took the three small lifeboats and dragged them across the ice. After two hours, they had traveled less than two miles. They were stranded and no one knew where they were.

Answers: 1b, 2d, 3a, 4c

Hands

Objective: Students will identify the main idea and supporting details of a reading passage.

Materials: Construction paper or blank paper, or use the hand template on page 160 (see example below)

What to Do: Have each student trace her hand on a piece of paper. In the palm of the hand outline, the student writes the main idea of the story or article. On each finger, she records a detail related to the main idea. For older students, use graphic organizers (see pages 130-131).

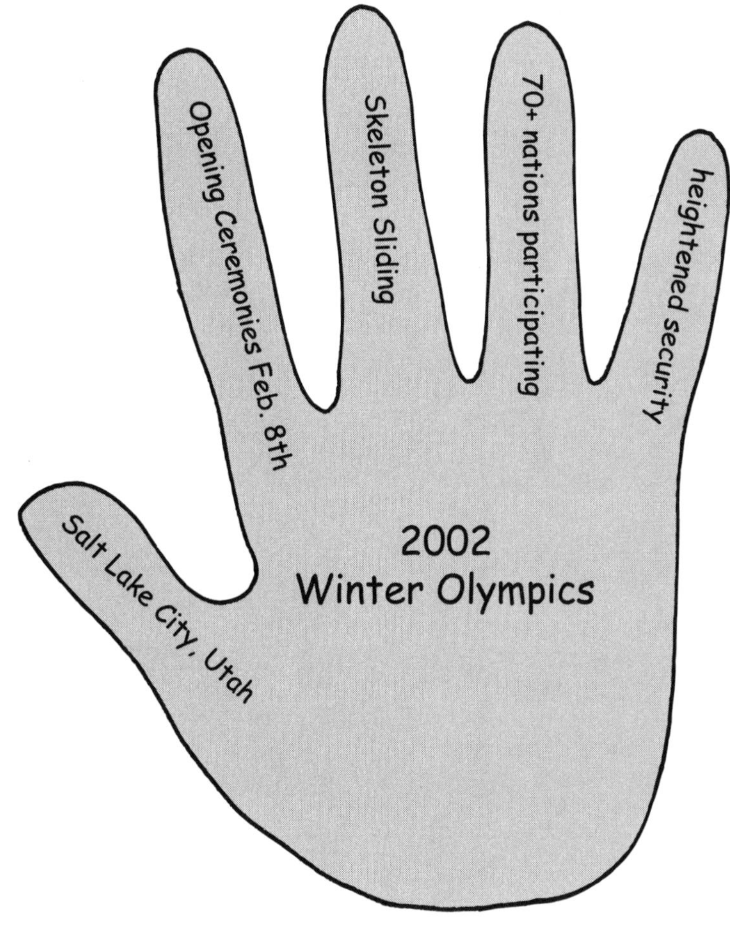

Use this hand outline to record the main idea and details of a reading passage. Write the main idea on the palm. Write each detail on a finger.

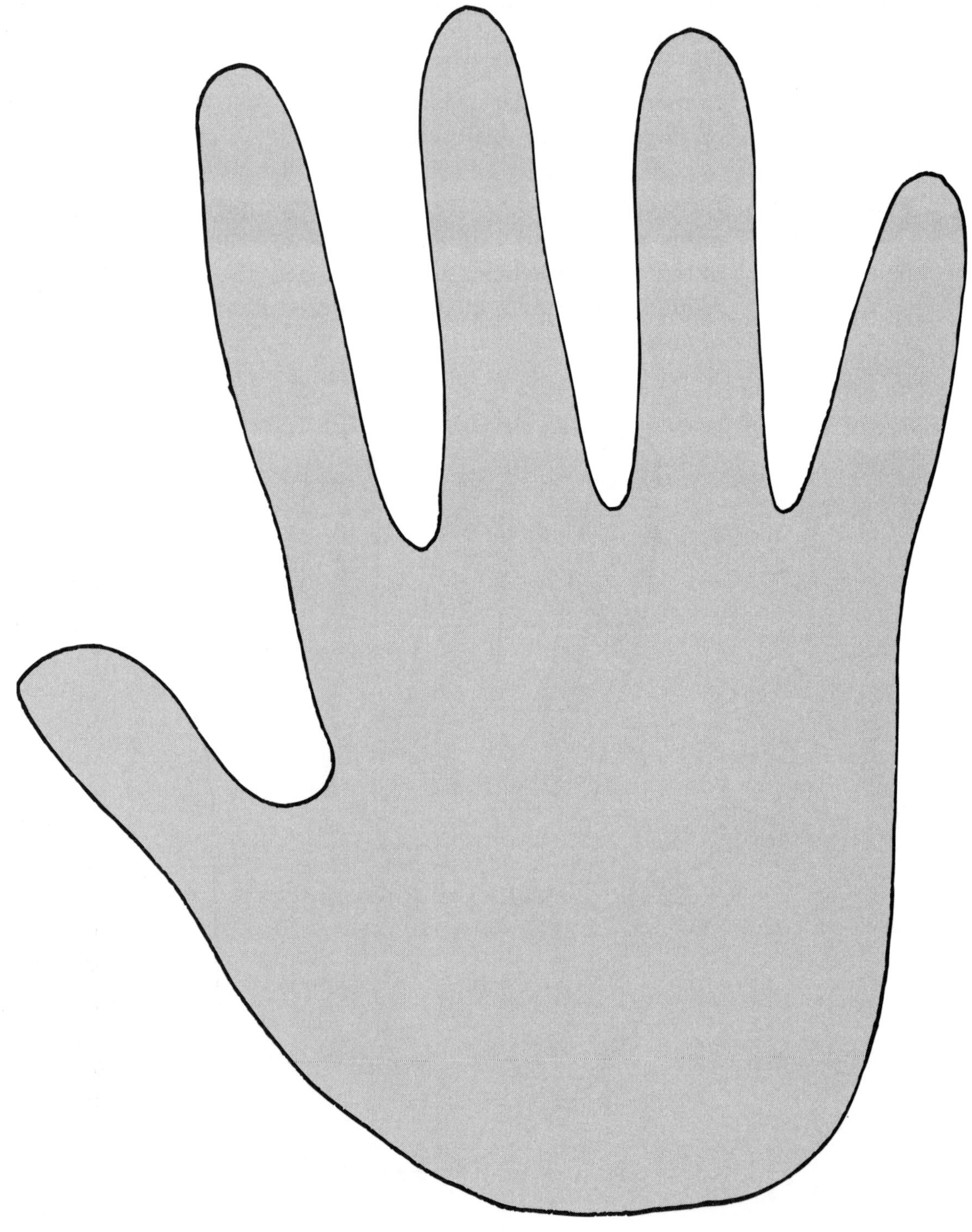

After-Reading Activities

Students must reflect upon and summarize what they have read for several reasons. Obviously, you want to know if your students understood what they read. Also, students can answer the questions they had before they started to read. In addition, reflecting upon what they have read deepens their knowledge of a specific topic and enhances their ability to make connections with literature.

If your students have participated in effective pre-reading and during-reading activities, paraphrasing, summarizing, and retelling activities will provide motivating ways to extend your students' reading comprehension.

➥ Paraphrasing Activities

You can have your students paraphrase (restate information in his own words) during and after a reading. Paraphrasing can be done at the sentence and/or the paragraph level. Some of the activities for determining the main idea can be modified for paraphrasing. For example, see Title It on page 156. Instead of having students use the provided titles, have them create their own titles by paraphrasing. Students can also practice paraphrasing by using the paragraphs that are provided.

➥ Summarizing/Retelling Activities

Once your students have completed their reading, it is important for them to be able to tell you/someone about the story or article, either orally or in writing. On the following pages, you will find a variety of activities to engage students in summarizing. Summarizing is the culmination of all the skills students engage in while they read, such as questioning and determining the main ideas. Retelling transforms summarizing into an oral expressive exercise that offers a great opportunity to instruct and practice public speaking skills, such as eye contact, tone of voice, and rate of speech. The activities on pages 164-166 provide examples of motivating ways to have your students retell information.

Sentence Jar

Objective: Students will put the main ideas of text into their own words.

Materials: Sentence strips (cut-up sentences from a news article or story)
Jar

What to Do: Cut up sentences from an article and put them in a jar. Have the students take turns pulling the sentences out of the jar and paraphrasing the information. You or your students can record the new sentences on sentence strips.

Two examples of original and paraphrased sentences are shown below.

Original sentence: Over the years, gray wolves that once populated the West were hunted to extinction.

New sentence: Gray Wolves in the West have been hunted to the point of extinction over the years.

Original sentence: Many of the wolves are wandering into ranchers' yards and devouring valuable livestock, including cattle and sheep.

New sentence: Wolves are killing cattle and sheep, which are two examples of the livestock that are valuable to ranchers.

Extension Activity

The students can sequence the sentences to create a cohesive summary.

Fables

Objective: Students will paraphrase the main ideas of fables in their own words.

Materials: Yolen, J. *A Sip of Aesop.* New York: Blue Sky Press, 1995.

What to Do: Fables are a great tool to practice paraphrasing. The language of fables can often be formal, so have your students retell the brief stories in their own words. Depending on the age and interests of your students, the group can also act out their retellings of the stories. Below is an example paraphrasing of the *Tortoise and the Hare* fable.

The Tortoise and the Hare

There once was a cocky rabbit who thought he was faster than anyone in the world. The rabbit challenged the slow, careful turtle to a race around the town.

On the day of the race, the rabbit teased the turtle, as the rabbit was sure he would win by a mile!

The race began, and the rabbit zipped ahead while the turtle maintained a slow but steady pace. The rabbit was so far ahead that he decided to take a little snooze. As he was sleeping soundly, the turtle sauntered by and won the race.

The moral of the story is **actions speak louder than words**.

Get the Facts, Jack

Objective: Students will write and orally summarize the important information of their reading.

Materials: One Get the Facts, Jack chart (page 148) per student, or copy this chart onto butcher block paper

Markers

What to Do: After a reading, have your students fill in the information on the Get the Facts, Jack chart. Next have your students number the facts on this chart in a logical sequence (see the example below). After each fact is numbered, the students should rewrite the facts into a paragraph.

Who Johnny Appleseed (2)	**What** planted apple trees (4)
Where all through the frontier (5)	**When** from the age of 25-75 (1)
Why He wanted to feed the people headed out West. (6)	**How** walked (3)

Paragraph: From the age of twenty-five to when he was seventy-five, Johnny Appleseed walked and planted apple trees all over the frontier. He planted the apple trees because he wanted to feed the people who were headed out West.

News Center

Objective: Students will orally summarize a current events article.

Materials: Summaries written from Get the Facts, Jack charts (see pages 148 and 164)

Handheld microphone

Butcher block paper

Markers

What to Do: Set up your classroom as a news center by making a banner.

Each student chooses and reports a current events story, including an introduction and a conclusion. This is a great opportunity to address public speaking skills, such as eye contact, tone of voice, rate of speech, etc. An example student report is written below.

"Hi, my name is Mary and I'm reporting for Classroom 24 News.

"Did you know that 2003 is the year of the Sheep?

"February 1st marks the beginning of the Chinese New Year. All over the country, many Chinese people will participate in parades, feasts, and festivities that bring in the New Year.

"I'm Mary, reporting from the Classroom 24 Newsroom."

Retelling Evaluations

Objective: Students will orally retell what they have read in a clear, logical sequence with appropriate eye contact.

Materials: Student summaries written from Get the Facts, Jack charts (see pages 148 and 164)

Copies of the Retelling Evaluation Form, below (one evaluation form per listener)

What to Do: Have the students use their summaries from the Get the Facts, Jack chart to retell their story to at least three other people. After listening to the summary, each listener completes a Retelling Evaluation Form.

Retelling Evaluation Form

Listen to ____________________ retell what he/she read. Check each box he/she used well. Write any comments and sign your name.

- ❑ introduction
- ❑ eye contact
- ❑ clear speaking voice
- ❑ conclusion

Comments ____________________________

____

____

____

____
signature

Retelling Evaluation Form

Listen to ____________________ retell what he/she read. Check each box he/she used well. Write any comments and sign your name.

- ❑ introduction
- ❑ eye contact
- ❑ clear speaking voice
- ❑ conclusion

Comments ____________________________

____

____

____

____
signature

Going Beyond the Reading

There are lots of great ways to extend what your students have learned while having fun with their reading material. Capitalize on the personalities and talents of your individual students. Take the opportunity to let them shine!

If you have singers or musicians in your class, encourage them to use music in a creative way to summarize a book. Writers in your class can change the story ending, write sequels, craft poems, write letters to the author, or create a journal page in the voice of a character. Artistically inclined students can do paintings, posters, comic strips, or Power Point presentations to use their creativity to go beyond their reading.

The following pages offer some ways to reinforce comprehension and encourage creativity at the same time.

Dear Diary,

Boy, I'm going to be in so much trouble when I get home! Today Mr. Krupps, my principal, found out that George and I put liquid soap in the band's instruments. What is the big deal? Everybody thought it was funny, well, almost everybody, and nobody got hurt. Plus, the game was really boring! It livened the place up! Mr. Krupps is a complete dud!!!

I'm dead meat. I'll write tomorrow, if I'm still alive.............

Harold

Puppet Shows

Objective: Students will generalize their understanding of fables (short stories that usually include animals that talk, and end with a moral or lesson) in order to write a script that tells an original fable.

Materials: Socks to make sock puppets
Poster board to make stick puppets
Felt, fabric, and any materials you can use to create puppets

What to Do: After completing your unit on the fables, have your students write their own fable as a group. Provide a model of the structure of a fable (e.g., animals, problem, resolution, lesson) that your students can use as they write. Once the script is complete, your students can begin to create their puppets and scenery. You can organize a puppet show event and invite other classes to attend!

Write a Sequel

Objective: Students will generalize their understanding of a story, the characters, and the plot to write a believable sequel to a story.

Materials:
Paper
Pencils
Books students have read
One copy of Write a Sequel (page 170) per student

What to Do: After your students have completed a book, discuss books that they have read that have sequels or are part of a series, such as *A Series of Unfortunate Events* by Lemony Snicket or the Harry Potter books by J.K. Rowling. Talk about what the books have in common and why book series captivate readers.

Help your students fill in the Write a Sequel chart about the book they just completed. Use the chart to help them plan, and ultimately write, a believable sequel to their books. Their books can be bound and displayed in the classroom or in the school's library. It may be fun to have your students write to the author with their ideas for a sequel!

Write a Sequel

Completed Book Title ______________________________

Characters ______________________________

____

Setting ______________________________

____

Plot ______________________________

____

Problem ______________________________

____

Resolution ______________________________

____

Sequel Book Title ______________________________

Characters ______________________________

____

Setting ______________________________

____

Plot ______________________________

____

Problem ______________________________

____

Resolution ______________________________

____

Drama Queen (or King)

Objective: Students will use their understanding of a character to role-play how the character would react in a given situation.

Materials: Situations written on index cards

What to Do: After reading a book, students choose the role of one of the main characters to portray. Each student picks a card, reads the situation, and then role-plays how her character would react in that particular situation. This role-play facilitates a discussion about character development and interpretation.

The example here shows role-playing based on the character Junie B. from the Junie B. Jones book series by Barbara Park.

Her teacher decides to give a pop quiz on rocks.

Dear Diary

Objective: Students will summarize the main events of a character's or a person's life in journal or diary form. They will transform the text from third-person to first-person as they record the events.

Materials: One journal or small notebook per student

Stories with strong characters, written in the third person, or biographies

What to Do: Students can do this activity after a book is completed or while they are still reading a book. Give each student a small journal or notebook. Have the student summarize the story by composing a journal that the main character may have written. The example below is based on the character Harold in the Captain Underpants series by Dav Pilkey.

Dear Diary,

Boy, I'm going to be in so much trouble when I get home! Today Mr. Krupps, my principal, found out that George and I put liquid soap in the band's instruments. What is the big deal? Everybody thought it was funny, well, almost everybody, and nobody got hurt. Plus, the game was really boring! It livened the place up! Mr. Krupps is a complete dud!!!

I'm dead meat. I'll write tomorrow, if I'm still alive.............

Harold

Comical Comprehension

Objective: Students will use their understanding of a story to create a comic strip based on what they read.

Materials: Completed books (novels, biographies, or nonfiction)
One copy of Comic Strip (page 174) per student

What to Do: After a student finishes a book or reading an article, have him create a comic strip that goes along with a specific event from the story. Be sure to explain that the student is not making up a situation, but taking an event from the story and summarizing the event in a dramatic or comical way. The example below is based on *Junie B. Jones and that Meanie Jim's Birthday*.

Extension Activity

Combine your student's comic strips together and create a funny pages section of your class newspaper titled *Comic Relief*.

Comic Strip

Create a comic strip that goes along with an event from what you read.

Title of Book ______________________________

Title of Comic Strip ______________________________ Illustrated by ______________________________

Memory Lane

Objective: Students will apply their questioning techniques and comprehension of the text to create a review activity based on the books they have read throughout the year.

Materials: Index cards

What to Do: After you complete a book with your class, have each student make up five questions about the book. You may want to structure this task so the students' questions are not too similar. For example, ask one group of students to focus on chapters one through three, another group on chapters four through six, etc. These questions could also include specific vocabulary from the readings.

Once the question-writing phase is complete, take a stroll down "Memory Lane." The great thing about this activity is that the pile of question cards will "grow" throughout the year as the students add more cards each time the class completes a book. This is a great warm-up activity for a class or end of class game.

Each student takes a turn drawing a question card from the pile and reading the question aloud. The rest of the students can raise their hands or write the answers down on scrap paper. Record points for right answers if you want to turn this activity into a game.

Extension Activity

Your students can create their own "Memory Lane" game boards to be used with the question cards. They can add their own game pieces, die, etc.

Appendix

On the next two pages, you will find examples of two motivational challenges for your students. These challenges are also great examples of ways you can encourage your students to read over weekends and vacations.

Reading Record

For the Reading Record (Appendix A, page 177), you can set a weekly reading goal or a vacation time goal of a certain number of pages. For example, on Monday, set a goal of 30 pages for your third-grade readers; if you have a class of mixed reading abilities, you can set individual goals. Have your students use the form to keep a daily record of how many pages they are reading. Add up the pages at the end of the week.

You can do the same thing for over a vacation. If your students meet the goal, you can have them visit your "prize box" or "sticker box." Another option is to have a celebration where everyone brings in their favorite reading and shares it with the class while enjoying a special treat.

Vacation Reading Challenge

The Vacation Reading Challenge (Appendix B, page 178), is a contract your students can sign before they go on vacation. Together, you and each student agree on a set number of pages (or books) to be read. Then sign the contract; the "reader" is the student and you are the "challenger." Before returning from break, each student should have an adult witness sign the contract to prove that the student has read the required number of pages over the vacation.

Again, it is motivating for your students to know that there will be a celebration (e.g., class breakfast, donut party) for all who complete the challenge. You can modify the model of the Vacation Reading Challenge to meet the needs of your students.

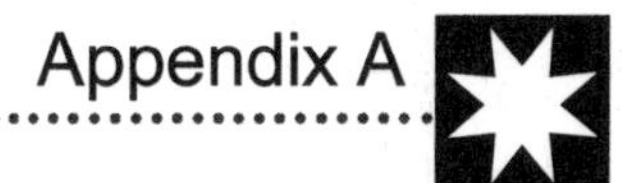

Reading Record

Record each reading on this log. Then write the total number of pages you read in the box at the bottom of this page.

Date	Book	Number of pages

Total number of pages →

Vacation Reading Challenge

I, ______________________________, accept the
name

reading challenge to read during vacation. I will read over 100 pages, complete this form, and return it to ______________________________ on
teacher's name

____________________.
date

My ____________________ will sign below as a
parent/guardian

witness that I met this reading challenge during my vacation.

Witness ______________________________

Reader ______________________________

Challenger ______________________________

Happy Reading!

References

Cunningham, P. M. (2000). *Phonics They Use.* New York: Addison-Wesley.

Johns, J. and Lenski, S. D. (1997). *Improving Reading.* Dubuque, Iowa: Kendall/Hunt Publishing Company.

Lyon, G. R. (1999). Keys to Successful Learning: A national summit on research in learning disabilities. New York: National Center for Learning Disabilities.

Ogle, D. M. (1986). The K-W-L: A teaching model that develops active reading of expository text. *The Reading Teacher, 29,* 564-70.

Reading Comprehension Games

There are many great commercial games that can be used to help build decoding, word-attack, and reading comprehension skills while keeping the kids motivated. Some of our favorites are listed here:

Balderdash, Gameworks Creations

Bingo

Boggle, Parker Bros.

Reading Comprehension Game, Elementary, LinguiSystems

Scattegories, Hasbro

Scrabble, Hasbro

Upwords, Hasbro

Vowel Scramble, LinguiSystems

Vowel Scramble 2, LinguiSystems

Word Building Dice

Word Scramble, LinguiSystems

Word Scramble 2, LinguiSystems

19-03-987654321

